International Trade Institutions

G. J. Lanjouw

translated
from the Dutch
by
ACE Translations

Longman
London and New York

Open University of the Netherlands
Heerlen

Longman Group UK Limited,
Longman House, Burnt Mill,
Harlow, Essex CM20 2JE, England
and Associated Companies throughout the world.

*Published in the United States of America
by Longman Publishing, New York*

First published 1995

ISBN 0 582 277647 PPR

British Library Cataloguing-in-Publication Data

A catalogue record for this book is
available from the British Library

Library of Congress Cataloging-in-Publication Data

Lanjouw, G. J.
    International trade institutions / G. J. Lanjouw.
        p.   cm.
    Includes bibliographical references and index.
    ISBN 0-582-27764-7
    1. International trade—Societies, etc. 2. International economic
relations—Societies, etc. 3. International agencies.   I. Title.
HF1371.L36   1996
382'.91—dc20   95-23081
                                                        CIP

Set by 8 in 10/12 Times New Roman
Produced through Longman Malaysia, PP

Contents

The International Business Programme

This volume, together with the volume by Dr A. F. P. Bakker, *International Financial Institutions* (Longman Group Ltd., 1995), and an accompanying study guide produced by the Netherlands' Open University (OU), forms an integrated 100 hour course, called 'International Economic Institutions'. This course has been specifically developed as part of a larger (1300 hour or 39 credit points) OU higher distance teaching programme on International Business. There are no formal pre-requisites to enter the programme; however, one has to recognise the programme's academic level. The course materials have been carefully designed for distance teaching purposes, which means that the student should be able to comprehend the course contents without additional educational tools.

The International Business Programme has been specifically designed for junior and mid-career professionals. After completion of the programme, the candidates are qualified to enter the European Master of Business Administration Programme which has been organised by a number of European distance teaching universities.

The International Business Programme centers around the following themes:

- International Economic Relations; main modules: Introduction to International Economics, International Trade
- Business Administration; main modules: International Financial Management and Accounting
- Management; main modules: International Human Resource Management, International Management I, Strategic Issues in Management in an European Context
- Institutions; main modules: International Economic Institutions, European Economic Integration

The International Business Programme is completed with a course called International Business Simulation, wherein students actively take part, as members of an international team of company executives, in an international computerized system simulation.

Although the International Business Programme has been designed as an intellectually and conceptually integrated whole, the various underlying modules of 100 hours (3 credit points) each can also be studied independently. Separate modules or sets of modules can be purchased at the Netherlands' Open University, either with or without the right to additional tutorial support or to take an official exam.

For more information, please contact:

Professor Catrinus J. Jepma or Mrs Elise Kamphuis
Co-ordinators, International Business Programme
Open University of the Netherlands, Department of Economics
PO Box 2960
6401 DL Heerlen
The Netherlands
Tel.: +31 45 762724
Fax.: +31 45 762123
E-mail: elise.kamphuis@ouh.nl

Preface

The idea for this book was conceived in the Faculty of Economics at the Open University of The Netherlands in Heerlen. It was felt that a textbook about international institutions in both Dutch and English was needed, which could be used in combination with A. F. P. Bakker's text *International Financial Institutions* (also available in Dutch and English versions). Together the two books form the basis of the International Economic Institutions course in the International Relations/ International Business Programme at the Open University. Some institutions, such as the EU and the OECD, are dealt with in both books to give the reader a complete picture of their function, this book gives references to relevant parts of *International Financial Institutions*.

The emphasis of this book is not on the technical aspects of the various institutions in the legal sense, but on their meaning for the economies of the countries involved and for the prosperity of the world as a whole.

In writing this book I have assumed that the reader has a basic knowledge of economics, that they are acquainted with the basic concepts of comparative advantage and price elasticities of demand and supply.

Throughout the conception and composition of this text, I have benefited from the useful input of several people. I am very grateful to Professors Henk Jager of the University of Amsterdam and Hans Visser of the Free University of Amsterdam, who acted as external referees of the International Economic Institutions course at the Open University. I would also like to thank Professor Catrinus Jepma and Mrs Elise Kamphuis of the Open University, Programme Leader and Course Team Leader respectively.

G. J. Lanjouw
Groningen, July 1995

Tables and figures

Abbreviations

ACM	Arab Common Market
APEC	Asian–Pacific Economic Co-operation
ANZCERTA	Australia–New Zealand Closer Economic Relations Trade Agreement
ASEAN	Association of South-East Asian Nations
CACM	Central American Common Market
CARICOM	Caribbean Community
CMEA/COMECON	Council for Mutual Economic Assistance
COCOM	Co-ordinating Committee for Export Controls
DAC	Development Assistance Committee (OECD)
EC	European Community
ECA	Economic Commission for Africa
ECE	Economic Commission for Europe
ECLAC	Economic Commission for Latin America and the Caribbean
ECO	Economic Co-operation Organisation
ECOSOC	Economic and Social Council (UN)
ECOWAS	Economic Community of West African States
ECSC	European Coal and Steel Community
ECWA	Economic Commission for Western Asia
EEA/EES	European Economic Area/Space
EEC	European Economic Community
EFTA	European Free Trade Association
EMU	Economic and Monetary Union
EPU	European Payments Union
ESCAP	Economic and Social Commission for Asia and the Pacific
EU	European Union
FAO	Food and Agriculture Organisation
GATT	General Agreement on Tariffs and Trade
GCC	Gulf Co-operation Council
IBEC	International Bank for Economic Co-operation

List of abbreviations

IBRD	International Bank for Reconstruction and Development (World Bank)
IEA	International Energy Agency
ILO	International Labour Organisation
IMF	International Monetary Fund
ITO	International Trade Organisation
LAFTA	Latin American Free Trade Association
LAIA	Latin American Integration Association
NAFTA	North American Free Trade Agreement
OECD	Organisation for Economic Co-operation and Development
OEEC	Organisation for European Economic Co-operation
OPEC	Organisation of Petroleum Exporting Countries
PTA	Preferential Trade Area
UNCED	UN Conference on Environment and Development
UNCTAD	UN Conference on Trade and Development
UNCTC	UN Centre on Transnational Corporations
UNEP	UN Environmental Program
UN	United Nations
WTO	World Trade Organisation

1 International economic organisations: the landscape

During and immediately after World War II the basis of a new international economic order was laid, establishing the institutional framework for international trade and financial relations in the post-war period, at least for countries which have based their economic system on the market mechanism co-ordinating the economic activities of various groups of economic agents.

Consultation on the post-war international economic order initially took place within the United Nations, where at first the primary concern was joining forces against the Axis powers, Germany, Italy and Japan. However, attention was also paid to the form of the post-war order. The foundations of the United Nations as a formalised international organisation were laid by the Charter signed in San Francisco in June 1945. In October of that same year the Charter was ratified by sufficient countries for the United Nations to be launched as an organisation. Subsequently, a system of international bodies developed to become what is generally known as the United Nations family. In the economic sphere the most important body is the Economic and Social Council (ECOSOC), which co-ordinates the work of a number of specialised agencies in the economic and social field.

It is noticeable that, although consultation on the post-war international economic order initially took place within the United Nations, the most significant international economic organisations were in fact eventually located outside the United Nations family. The International Monetary Fund was set up as a result of the United Nations Monetary and Financial Conference of July 1944 – better known as the Bretton Woods Conference after the place in New Hampshire, USA, where it was held – but gained independent status, although it is formally a specialised agency of the UN. The independent position of the Fund is reflected among other things in the rules on members' voting rights, which differ from the general principle applied in the UN of unweighted votes, whereby all countries have the same influence over decision-making. In the IMF, votes are weighted and correspond to the quota contributed to the Fund, which can be regarded as an approximation of the economic importance of the country concerned.

The organisation dealing with international trade which was intended to be set up as a specialised agency within the United Nations family, namely the International Trade Organisation, was not established in the end. What was left was the General

Agreement on Tariffs and Trade (GATT) of 1947, which had no formal relationship with the United Nations. In this agreement, a more limited set of trade policy principles was formulated.

The IMF and the GATT are the two most important international organisations of the post-war international economic order, which is therefore also known as the GATT–IMF order.

In consultations on what form the post-war international economic order should take, an important factor was the concern to avoid a repeat of what had happened to international economic relations between the wars. This period, especially in the 1930s, is noted for its beggar-thy-neighbour policy, which means that countries tried to transfer to others the economic problems afflicting them during the Great Depression. In trade policy this is reflected in the sharp increase in import duties and the erection of other trade barriers. The very high tariffs introduced by the United States in 1930 under the Smoot–Hawley Act had an important place in this process. In the sphere of exchange-rate policy, attempts were made to secure artificial competitive advantages by means of depreciation, but these attempts failed because other countries responded by depreciating their currencies, too. This led to disastrous competitive depreciations. The result of the beggar-thy-neighbour practices was that the world economy sank even further into the mire as international trade collapsed.

The lesson which is learnt from the inter-war period is that countries need to agree rules on how they conduct their international economic policy and that they should aim at freedom of international transactions. The changed attitude towards international economic relations is very clear in the case of the United States, where – in 1934 – the option was introduced of giving the President extensive powers over trade policy from time to time; before that, Congress had played the main role in this sphere. This made it easier to remove trade policy from the influence of national interest groups, which are readily inclined to demand protectionist measures. From that time on, the United States also took the lead in consultations on a liberal international economic order.

The aim of a liberal economic order, apart from being expressed in negative terms as preventing history from repeating itself, can also be stated in positive terms as the creation of a framework within which countries can specialise in production according to their comparative advantage. Thus, the means of production can be allocated in the best possible way among the countries of the world, and world prosperity can be maximised.

This book will discuss international economic institutions of the post-war world economy, though it will only cover institutions in the sphere of international trade and trade policy.[1] These are institutions which affect the international trade policies of individual nations, particularly in imposing restrictions on those policies, and not bodies which are themselves concerned with specific international trade activities. For the participating countries it is in fact a question of sacrificing part of their national freedom to decide policy, in the belief that international co-operation offers such great advantages that the sacrifice will eventually prove worthwhile.

---

[1] International financial organisations are dealt with in A. F. P. Bakker, *International financial institutions*, Harlow, 1995 (first published in Amsterdam, 1992).

One effect of confining the book to international trade institutions is that, while the GATT is discussed in detail (in Chapter 2), the other pillar of the post-war international economic order, the IMF, is not mentioned further. However, one aspect of the IMF which is important for international trade will be considered here: the provisions contained in its Articles of Agreement concerning the convertibility of currencies. If international trade transactions are to take place unhindered, not only must the international movement of goods be as free as possible from trade policy restrictions; it is also important to be able to arrange settlement for international trade transactions. Thus, an importer who has to pay his foreign supplier in the latter's currency must actually be able to purchase that currency. And an exporter receiving payment from his foreign customer in the latter's currency will generally want to convert it into his own currency. This necessitates freely convertible currencies. Under the IMF Articles of Agreement, convertibility is compulsory only for transactions shown on the current account of the balance of payments (current-account convertibility). Restrictions are allowed on capital movements, e.g. in order to prevent speculation. This limitation on convertibility was also influenced by the experience of the inter-war period, when destabilising capital movements, then often referred to as hot money flows, occurred from time to time.

The importance of currency convertibility as defined in the IMF Articles is also that it creates the possibility of a multilateral trade system in which bilateral trade surpluses and deficits can exist because the resulting currency balances can be converted and used elsewhere. Thus, apart from the liberalisation of trade policy which takes place primarily in the GATT/WTO, convertibility is an essential element of the liberal post-war international economic order.

In practice, this element is often missing. There is a provision in the IMF Articles permitting a transitional period before convertibility: the length of this period is unlimited, so that the currencies of many countries, especially developing countries, are still not convertible.

Another important post-war international organisation, the International Bank for Reconstruction and Development (IBRD), commonly known as the World Bank, is also left out of account in this book. This organisation which, like the IMF, was established as a result of the Bretton Woods Conference, was geared in the first instance to financing the reconstruction of the European economies ravaged by war. As time went by, the sphere of activities gradually shifted towards financing projects and programmes in developing countries. The World Bank, therefore, together with other institutions performing a related function, such as regional development banks, has a significant role in international trade for developing countries, in financing part of those countries' imports. However, as stated earlier, that direct involvement in international trade is not what this book is about.

As will be amply evident later on in this book, the idea of a liberal international economic order in the period after World War II came under pressure from time to time, particularly in the 1970s with the rise of the 'new protectionism'. Nevertheless, as shown by Table 1.1, the growth in international trade in subsequent periods always exceeded the growth of world output. This pattern was evident both in periods when world output was growing fast and when growth was depressed. It indicates that the

Table 1.1 Growth of world trade and world output; average annual growth rates, 1960–90

	1960–70 %	1970–80 %	1980–90 %
Growth in the volume of world trade	8.5	5	4
Growth in the volume of world output	6	4	2.5

Source: GATT, *International Trade*, various issues

world economy continued to become increasingly internationalised, with an ever-increasing proportion of world output being traded internationally.

In 1964 the United Nations Conference on Trade and Development (UNCTAD) was added to the world's international economic organisations. This organisation, which will be discussed in Chapter 3, deals with the international economic problems of developing countries. Another major new organisation in the UN family which will be covered in Chapter 3 is the United Nations Commission on Transnational Corporations, which is concerned with the issue of multinational or, in UN terminology, transnational corporations. The role which the UN plays in tackling environment questions is also considered.

As well as global international economic organisations there are also regional organisations. Thus, the United Nations has regional economic commissions for each part of the world; these are also discussed in Chapter 3. However, more important in this connection are the regional economic co-operative associations which aim at economic integration in one form or another. These have become more significant of late, so much so that some people are afraid that the world economy will fragment, with an increasing number of inward-looking blocs threatening the multilateral international economic system. The most important regional economic integration associations are discussed in Chapter 6.

A totally different kind of regional economic integration association, such as those between countries with a centrally planned economy, is discussed in Chapter 7. The same chapter also deals with other institutions concerned with international trade by countries whose domestic currency is not convertible. This refers not to arrangements made by international economic organisations, but to matters covered by the broader concept of institutions. It also explains why the title of this book refers to institutions rather than organisations. In particular, the term 'institutions' is broader because, apart from *official* international organisations, it also covers spontaneously developed forms of international transactions such as counter-trade in the case of countries with a non-convertible currency.

An international economic organisation which began as a regional co-operative association between West European countries but was later expanded to include other industrial countries, the Organisation for Economic Co-operation and Development (OECD), is discussed in Chapter 4. Although the members of this organisation are the more prosperous countries of the world, it is not accurate to regard the OECD purely as promoting the interests of the rich nations, because it also performs an important function in co-ordinating the member countries' development co-operation effort.

Another totally different kind of international institution is the arrangements concerning international trade in primary commodities, whether or not in the form of commodity agreements between exporting and importing countries. These are covered in Chapter 5.

Bibliography

Gardner, R. N., *Sterling–Dollar Diplomacy in Current Perspective: The Origins and the Prospects of Our International Economic Order*, New York, 1980.

Richards, J. H., *International Economic Institutions*, London, 1970.

Spero, J. E, *The Politics of International Economic Relations*, London, 1990.

United Nations, *Everybody's United Nations: A Handbook on the Work of the United Nations*, New York, 1986.

2   From the General Agreement on Tariffs and Trade (GATT) to the World Trade Organisation (WTO)

2.1   History

As stated in the first chapter, in the post-war international economic system the original intention was to set up, alongside the international monetary and financial organisations (the IMF and the World Bank), an international organisation in the sphere of international trade, in the form of the International Trade Organisation (ITO). Discussions on this resulted in the Havana Charter in 1948, intended to form the basis of the ITO, which would deal with many questions relating to international trade. Apart from a section on trade policy, the Havana Charter also has sections on employment and economic activity, economic development and reconstruction, restrictive business practices and international commodity agreements. In the end the ITO was not set up, largely because it was not ratified by the American Congress. Since the establishment of the first international organisations immediately after the war, the US attitude to international co-operation has become markedly more reticent.

As long ago as 1947 in Geneva, in anticipation of the formation of the ITO, the General Agreement on Tariffs and Trade (GATT) was concluded. Under this agreement, the countries concerned undertake to make specific concessions on trade policy. The GATT also included many of the trade policy provisions which were introduced in the process of drawing up the Havana Charter. The agreement was intended to apply in the transitional phase up to establishment of the ITO. However, when the ITO was not set up, the GATT remained in force. One peculiar consequence of this background was that the GATT, being an agreement and not a real international organisation, did not have member countries but contracting parties, though the GATT did operate subsequently as a *de facto* international organisation from a permanent secretariat in Geneva. In 1960 a further step forward was taken with the creation of the Council of Representatives, a body at ambassador level meeting roughly nine times a year and deciding on both routine questions and urgent matters. As we shall see later on in this chapter, as a result of the Uruguay Round the GATT was converted on 1 January 1995 into the World Trade Organisation (WTO), thus becoming a fully fledged international organisation.

2.2 The GATT principles

The GATT, as an international agreement, is based on three principles:

1. *Non-discrimination*. This is the basic principle of the GATT. It is expressed in two ways, namely in the principles of most-favoured-nation (MFN) treatment in international trade and of national treatment of foreign products. MFN treatment means that individual contracting parties must treat all other contracting parties equally in their international trade relations with them. Thus, if a country which is a party to the GATT grants a trade concession, such as a reduced import duty, to another GATT country, that concession automatically applies to all other contracting parties, too. The principle of national treatment means that, apart from the application of trade policy measures such as the levying of import duties, imported products must be treated in the same way as home-produced goods. For example, this means that they must be subject to the same indirect taxes.

   There are exceptions to the principle of non-discrimination. An important exception to the most-favoured-nation principle is that discriminatory treatment is allowed within free-trade areas and customs unions, such as the European Union (see Chapter 6). Another exception concerns developing countries, which, under Part IV (entitled 'Trade and Development') added to the GATT in 1965, can receive preferential treatment for imports of their products into industrial countries. This opens the way to the Generalised System of Preferences (see the section on UNCTAD in Chapter 3).

2. *Reciprocity*. This principle means that if one GATT contracting party makes a trade concession, other contracting parties should make equivalent concessions. The intention is that this should balance the advantages and disadvantages of trade liberalisation. Although in theory it is advantageous for a country to permit free trade regardless of whether other countries do the same, in practice countries regard reducing barriers to imports as a concession which should be reciprocated by other countries.

   The principle of reciprocity concerns not only the granting of concessions but also their withdrawal. In that case, too, other countries can restore the balance by withdrawing concessions in turn, or demanding compensatory concessions.

   It should be noted that it is not only tariff reductions that are regarded as a concession: tariff binding is viewed in the same way. This means entering into an obligation not to increase the tariffs concerned. It allows the trading partners of the country in question to be certain of the trade policy treatment of the products in question, at least as far as tariffs are concerned.

   There are also exceptions to the principle of reciprocity. The most important is that developing countries are not required to reciprocate. This exemption is based on Part IV of the GATT, as was the one mentioned under point 1 concerning developing countries.

3. *Prohibition on trade restrictions other than tariffs*. In principle, trade restrictions other than tariffs, particularly direct interference in international trade such as

quantitative restrictions limiting imports to a set maximum, are prohibited. Tariffs are a transparent means of restricting trade because tariff information is freely available. Moreover, tariffs have the advantage that they conform to the market, which means that markets are influenced but their operation is not affected, as would be the case with a quantitative restriction. Another consideration is that it is easier to negotiate on tariffs, and especially on their reduction, than on other measures which are often more difficult to quantify. These include qualitative measures such as specific procedures which must be followed on the importation of goods. It is difficult to apply a percentage reduction to these as can be done with tariffs. The other trade policy measures, known as non-tariff measures, will be discussed later in this chapter.

There are also exceptions to this principle, including the provision for direct intervention in international trade in the case of balance-of-payments problems.

2.3 The trade liberalisation negotiations up to and including the Kennedy Round (1947–67)

Once the GATT had been set up as an international agreement at the same time as an international commitment to tariff reductions, there followed a whole series of negotiation rounds on trade liberalisation. The Kennedy Round which lasted from

---

Box 2.1: The GATT rounds of negotiations

Up to the creation of the WTO there have been eight rounds of GATT negotiations on the liberalisation of world trade.

period	place	number of countries taking part at the start of the round
1947	Geneva	23
1949	Annecy	13
1951	Torquay	38
1956	Geneva	26
1960–1	Geneva (Dillon Round)	26
1964–7	Geneva (Kennedy Round)	62
1973–9	Geneva (Tokyo Round)	102
1986–93	Geneva (Uruguay Round)	105

Source: GATT, *GATT: What it is, what it does*, Geneva, 1991.

Over the years the rounds have expanded in both number of participants and range of subjects covered. According to newspaper reports at the time the Uruguay Round was concluded (end of 1993), the then GATT Director General, Peter Sutherland, wondered whether the negotiation process was not becoming too complicated and whether, in the future World Trade Organisation, there should not be much more negotiation by specific topics.

1964 to 1967 is often taken as a dividing line, because the negotiation techniques applied in the first five rounds before the Kennedy Round differed from those thereafter. In the first series of rounds, negotiations took place bilaterally on a product-by-product basis, with countries negotiating with one another on those products for which they were the principal suppliers to one another's markets. This rule for the negotiation process was known as the principal-supplier rule. Under the most-favoured-nation clause, the results of the bilateral negotiations also apply to trading partners of the two countries. The various bilateral negotiations are therefore connected, which makes it complicated for the countries to obtain an overall picture of the concessions granted and obtained. According to the principle of reciprocity, these should balance.

Because of the complexity of the negotiations in the first five rounds, an attempt was made to simplify them. The Kennedy Round was started with the much simpler aim of achieving linear tariff reductions, meaning that all participating countries would reduce their tariffs on the whole range of industrial products by a certain percentage – 50 per cent was envisaged. It would then only be necessary to negotiate on the exceptions. In the end, this technique was only used in the negotiations between the most important industrial countries, or groups of industrial countries. The ultimate outcome was below target, with an average tariff reduction of approximately 35 per cent, but it was nevertheless an important step in the process of trade liberalisation. The difference between the starting point of a 50 per cent tariff reduction and what was actually achieved is partly to do with the fact that countries with tariffs which are already low in absolute terms are not prepared to apply the same percentage reduction as countries whose tariffs are still much higher and which thus have more room for manoeuvre. This often applied to talks between the European Community and the United States, in which the European Community attacked the high American tariffs on some products. In this kind of case, the result was that a harmonisation of tariffs was agreed whereby high tariffs were reduced more sharply than low ones.

The Kennedy Round also made a start on negotiations over other trade barriers, the 'non-tariff barriers'. The results were less impressive here. Another new feature was the desire to make a determined effort to tackle the liberalisation of trade in the agricultural sector during the Kennedy Round. Agriculture was initially excluded from the GATT, mainly because of the Americans' desire to continue protecting their own agriculture. With the introduction of a highly protectionist Common Agricultural Policy in the European Community, the American attitude changed and they wanted the agricultural sector to be included in GATT negotiations after all. However, the Kennedy Round actually achieved very little in the agricultural sphere.

The Kennedy Round also paid particular attention to reducing trade barriers in relation to developing countries. On this point, too, the eventual results were disappointing. The average tariff reduction on products important to developing countries is less than on products from the developed countries. One reason for this is the below-average tariff reductions on products from the textile and clothing sectors, in which the developing countries generally have a strong position.

In all, the Kennedy Round's main achievement lay in reducing tariffs on more advanced industrial products which are primarily of importance to industrial countries.

2.4 The Tokyo Round (1973–9)

After the Kennedy Round there was a pause in international talks on trade liberalisation. It was 1973 before approval of the Tokyo Declaration heralded the start of a new round of negotiations. This was initially called the Nixon Round, but after Nixon was forced to resign the US presidency it was renamed the Tokyo Round. The intention was to conclude the negotiations in 1975, but in the end it was 1979 before they could be successfully completed. Compared with the Kennedy Round, there was a shift of emphasis in that negotiations on tariffs were relatively less important and negotiations on non-tariff barriers to international trade gained in significance.

During the negotiations six main groups were formed on the basis of subject definitions: the main results of each are discussed below.

1. *Tropical products.* The industrial countries made substantial concessions on certain categories of tropical products; for other products, particularly those which had to compete with goods produced by the industrial countries themselves (e.g. sugar), the results were substantially less.

2. *Tariffs.* Since the Kennedy Round had already introduced considerable reductions in tariffs, various participants objected to a further linear tariff reduction. Instead, it was eventually decided to apply a tariff reduction formula which would also lead to tariff harmonisation. This is based on the Swiss formula, as it is called:

$$Z = \frac{A \, X}{A + X}$$

in which Z is the absolute level of the tariff after reduction, X is the tariff before reduction and A a figure to be agreed between 14 and 16. Taking the value of A as 14, as in the original Swiss proposal, a 10 per cent tariff would be reduced by almost 42 per cent, while a 20 per cent tariff would drop by over 55 per cent. For the industrial countries, this meant that tariffs were reduced by an average of one third.

3. *Non-tariff measures.* Reducing tariffs increases the relative importance of non-tariff measures influencing international trade. This means both measures aimed directly at restricting international trade and measures which have a different primary purpose but which also affect international trade. It is particularly measures in this last category that can be abused or misused to protect national interests. That is why the Tokyo Round agreed codes of conduct for a number of categories of non-tariff measures. This concerned the following five areas:

Box 2.2: The Poitiers effect

A famous example of an 'administrative procedure' used to restrict imports was the arrangement concerning the import of video recorders into France, introduced in October 1982 after a period of strong growth in imports of such equipment from Japan. In future, the recorders had to enter France via an understaffed customs office in Poitiers, which was already an out-of-the-way place. The instructions for use had to be carefully checked to see if they were written in French, and recorders were taken apart in order to check whether they were actually made in the stated country of origin. In this way the French in fact succeeded in substantially reducing imports of video recorders: the volume of imports declined from 64,000 per month to only 10,000. After a series of complaints, not only by Japan but also by other EC countries, the French government reversed the measure, but not until the European Commission had concluded an agreement with Japan 'voluntarily' restricting Japanese exports of video recorders to the EC.

Source: World Bank, *World Development Report 1987*, New York, 1987, p. 141.

- customs valuation. This entails ascertaining the value of goods at the border as the basis for levying tariffs. The purpose of the code of conduct is to achieve a 'fair, uniform and neutral system' of customs valuation.
- government procurement. The purpose of the code in this area is to limit the scope for governments to give preference to domestic companies in their procurement. The code provides for a number of exceptions, e.g. for the acquisition of military equipment.
- import licensing procedures. The intention of the code is that these should not be allowed to operate as additional restrictions on trade.
- subsidies and countervailing duties. This was one of the most important areas covered by the Tokyo Round, and the negotiations were laborious. The code interprets certain GATT articles in more detail. Apart from the existing prohibition on export subsidies for industrial products, agreements were now also concluded on the avoidance of domestic subsidies which might lead to distortions of competition. Rules were also formulated to prevent unnecessarily restrictive counter-measures against foreign subsidies, known as countervailing duties.
- technical barriers to trade. The code in this area aims to prevent technical rules and standards relating to products, e.g. those imposed on health or safety grounds, from leading to unnecessary restrictions on trade.

4. *Agriculture.* As in the Kennedy Round, the agricultural sector was again dealt with separately. And, once again, the results were not very impressive: the major confrontation over agricultural policy was not to come until the subsequent Uruguay Round. However, it was agreed that countries would exercise restraint in granting export subsidies on agricultural products: these subsidies must not lead to

countries securing more than an equitable share in world exports of the products concerned.

5. *Sectoral approach.* The intention of this was to achieve radical liberalisation of trade in specific sectors, as regards both tariffs and non-tariff barriers. Agreement on total trade liberalisation was only reached for one sector, namely the civil aircraft sector.

6. *Safeguards.* This refers to temporary trade restrictions in a particular sector based on Article XIX of the GATT, for the purpose of preventing market disruption by a sharp increase in imports. In trade policy practice, these measures appear to be little used because they carry with them certain conditions derived from the basic principles of the GATT. Thus, it is regarded as a disadvantage, particularly by the EC, that the measures must be applied on a non-discriminatory basis; the EC is in favour of allowing selective application, i.e. directing the measures at those trading partners regarded as the main sources of the market disruption, or the 'most troublesome' competitors. The chief opponents of the EC are the developing countries, which are afraid that allowing selective application will eliminate a major restraint on the imposition of import restrictions in the industrial world, and that they will be the principal victims. In the end, the Tokyo Round did not reach any agreement on the safeguards.

Overall, however, the Tokyo Round did represent a further step towards the liberalisation of trade, with the emphasis shifting away from tariff reduction and towards the liberalisation of other trade policy measures. Just as in previous rounds, the focus was on liberalising trade in industrial products important to industrial countries. Developing countries benefited substantially less, although the promotion of their trade interests was again one of the stated objectives of the round.

2.5 The rise of the 'new protectionism'

The fact that the Tokyo Round lasted longer than planned shows in itself that the post-war process of international trade liberalisation did not go entirely smoothly. At first this was thought to be merely because other barriers in the form of non-tariff restrictions were more visible following the reduction in tariffs. The metaphor applied here was of trade liberalisation representing the draining of a swamp. The reduction in tariffs symbolised letting the water level fall, uncovering what was below the surface in the form of non-tariff barriers. However, it gradually became clear that protection by non-tariff measures was steadily increasing, so the expression 'new protectionism' became commonplace. This term is used in various ways: one interpretation is that it refers to the use of new trade policy instruments which, though not in all cases contrary to the letter of the GATT, are contrary to its spirit. In this connection people talk of grey-area measures. A characteristic example is 'voluntary' export restraint (VER). This means restraint on exports by the exporting country, under pressure from an importing country experiencing what is considered too sharp a rise in imports of a particular product. The fact that the importing country applies pressure indicates that the restraint is not really voluntary. The question is why countries resort to such measures. One important reason is that the safeguards under Article XIX of the GATT, which are really supposed to be applied in cases where imports disrupt the market, are used less and less in practice because of the conditions attached to them (see also the previous section on the Tokyo Round). Contrary to frequent assertions, 'voluntary' export restraint also breaches the GATT rules, but does not lead to complaints to the GATT because VER was set up by the exporting countries themselves. Thus, there is no way that the GATT can take action against these measures.

But this still does not explain why countries undertake to apply the GATT rules and participate in GATT negotiations on trade liberalisation while at the same time going through all sorts of contortions in order to continue applying protectionist measures. This brings us to the question: why the new protectionism? Some people regard the new protectionism as a consequence of the increasingly important role of governments in the economic process during the post-war period, particularly intervention for the purpose of establishing a 'welfare state', an idea sometimes popularly called government care 'from the cradle to the grave'. One important function of the government is to provide security for its citizens, for example in the employment protection sphere, by imposing restrictions on dismissal procedures. According to some writers, this kind of government policy fossilises economic structures and, in the trade policy sphere, leads to measures which protect the home market against foreign competition.[1] This interpretation is not undisputed, because there are, for instance, countries where the government plays a very prominent role in the national economy but where a spirit of liberalism nevertheless prevails in trade policy.

Another more common explanation of the rise of the new protectionism is based on the shifts taking place in the international division of labour. This means in particular the rise of the Newly Industrialising Economies[2] such as the south-east Asian 'tigers' or 'dragons', Hong Kong, South Korea, Singapore and Taiwan. From the early 1960s they have been developing into formidable competitors with the established industrial nations, concentrating first on labour-intensive industrial products such as textiles and clothing, footwear and wooden products. Their low wages give these countries a comparative advantage in this type of product. In the 1970s, in particular, when the world economy suffered from a cyclical downturn following the first oil crisis, demands for protection against imports from the Newly Industrialising Economies became ever louder in the industrial countries, the main argument being the detrimental effect on employment. Empirical research has shown that the impact of imports from developing countries on employment in industrial country sectors competing with imports is slight in comparison with the influence of other factors such as changes in the productivity of labour.[3] Should we nevertheless wish to apply protection in order to preserve employment, we

---

[1] This view is evident for instance in M. B. Krauss, The New Protectionism: The Welfare State and International Trade, New York, 1978.

[2] The countries in question were originally labelled Newly Industrialising Countries by the OECD (see Chapter 4). Later this group was renamed, one reason being that one of the members, Taiwan, was not officially recognised as a country.

[3] See for example D. Greenaway, International Trade Policy: From Tariffs to the New Protectionism, London and Basingstoke, 1983, Chapter 11.

should be aware that this is associated with very high costs. The World Bank's *World Development Report 1987* surveys research into the costs to the consumer of preserving jobs by protectionism. In that connection the record is held by a number of British factories producing video recorders. Research on this sector has shown that it costs British consumers about £80,000 to preserve a single job for one year![4]

In explaining the rise of the new protectionism, the preceding paragraph concentrated on protectionism directed against developing countries and particularly the Newly Industrialising Economies within that group. However, it is not correct to see the new protectionism just as something taking place between industrial and developing countries. In the industrial world, too, in trade relations between the EC, the US and Japan, there are numerous examples of new protectionist measures.

An increasingly common phenomenon in the argument in favour of protectionism is the accusation that other countries are not applying the concept of 'fair trade' as they should. Although fair trade sounds like something that no one could object to, the way in which it is interpreted is sometimes highly dubious. One example in this connection is the way in which the term 'reciprocity' is interpreted differently from its meaning in the GATT. As already described, under the GATT the term 'reciprocity' refers to balance in trade policy concessions in international negotiations; in other words, changes in the use of trade policy instruments, the clearest example being the reduction of import tariffs by a particular percentage. This form of reciprocity is therefore known as first-difference reciprocity, 'first-difference' referring to the fact that changes in protection are involved.[5] In contrast the term 'reciprocity' as used – especially in the United States – by those who advocate 'fair trade', means integral reciprocity in the sense that markets are to be equally open to one another. Starting with the idea that 'the American market is the most open in the world', the belief is that other countries should practise the same openness in order to create a 'level playing field'. The danger of this approach lies mainly in what happens when attempts are made to implement it. The practical interpretation often takes the form of demanding equilibrium in the bilateral trade balance, and sometimes even in individual sectors of the trade balance. In this last case it is stipulated, for example, that if Japan exports cars to the United States leading to a certain amount of export receipts, Japan must import American cars to the same value to achieve reciprocity. This interpretation is at odds with the idea of a multilateral trade system and specialisation on the basis of comparative advantages, which forms the foundation of the GATT/WTO. In such a system, bilateral surpluses or deficits in the trade balance between countries are acceptable so long as the overall trade balance position of countries is in equilibrium.

A similar interpretation of 'fair trade' is evident in the American–Japanese Structural Impediments Initiative launched in 1989. Although the intention is to detect and subsequently eliminate structural impediments to bilateral trade, the project also appears to extend to matters such as government spending on infrastructure, said to be

---

[4] D. Greenaway and B. Hindley, *What Britain Pays for Voluntary Export Restraints,* Thames Essay No. 43, London, 1985, p. 59. The figure relates to the year 1983.

[5] This terminology is used in particular by J. Bhagwati. See, for instance, his *Protectionism*, Cambridge (Mass.) and London, 1988, p. 36.

too low in Japan, and the savings ratio, said to be too high. The idea behind this is that these factors also affect trade and hence the imbalance in bilateral trade between Japan and the United States. The danger of this approach is that, if taken to extremes, it could mean that all factors which affect trade are neutralised, ultimately eliminating the possibility of mutually advantageous trade between countries.[6]

We are bound to conclude that there is no single, straightforward reason for the new protectionism, but rather a combination of reasons: structural shifts in the international division of labour, cyclical movements in economic activity and a diminished willingness to adjust the production structure in industrial countries, plus a misinterpretation of the meaning of trade balance surpluses and deficits. In this regard, we might also mention the influence of exchange-rate movements, the example of the strong dollar in the first half of the 1980s being the one that most stirs the imagination. The strong dollar severely weakened the competitive position of American industry on the home market and abroad, leading to strong pressure for protectionist measures, on the apparent assumption that the deteriorating position was primarily due to 'unfair' foreign trade practices rather than the strength of the dollar.

2.6 The Uruguay Round (1986–93)

In September 1986 the desire to halt the rise of the new protectionism led to the launch of a new round of negotiations in Punta del Este, Uruguay, which subsequently became known as the Uruguay Round. A very comprehensive agenda was drawn up for the negotiations, which were meant to be concluded in four years; agreements were also reached to prevent any further increase in protection (referred to as 'standstill') and to reverse existing protectionist measures contrary to the GATT rules immediately (referred to as 'rollback').

The Uruguay Round had various features introduced since the Tokyo Round. One important new element was the attention paid to the liberalisation of international trade in services. Production of services represents a growing proportion of total economic activity, especially in industrial countries, so that the liberalisation of this sector is becoming ever more important for those countries. The GATT rules had not hitherto covered trade in services, which differs from trade in goods in a number of ways. For example, in order to provide services to other countries, it is often necessary for the supplier to be physically present in the customer country; for instance, in the case of services by banks and insurance companies. This means that international trade in this sector has far more significant consequences for the countries of destination. The GATT principle of particular relevance here is that of national treatment, i.e. foreign service companies should be able to operate on the same terms as their domestic competitors.

---

[6] See for example J. Bhagwati, *The World Trading System at Risk*, New York, 1991, pp. 21–2.

As regards the negotiations on trade in goods, an important new feature was that negotiations on liberalisation of international trade in agricultural products, which had only yielded only marginal results in previous rounds, were now tackled more drastically. Thus, the Punta del Este Declaration referred to phased reduction in the negative effects of the use of all direct and indirect subsidies and other measures directly or indirectly influencing trade in agricultural products.

The safeguards on which no agreement was reached in the Tokyo Round also remained on the agenda. Adaptation of the rules on this point is important if protection measures introduced outside the GATT rules are to be brought within the framework of the GATT. This was explicitly stated as an aim for the textiles and clothing sector where bilateral agreements between exporting and importing countries on 'voluntary' export restraint had applied under the Multifibre Agreement. More generally, the GATT system itself also came under discussion, again with the aim of counteracting the proliferation of protectionism outside the GATT rules. Here it was a question of strengthening the GATT as an international organisation, especially as regards supervision of the trade policy of the contracting parties.

The Punta del Este Declaration again vowed that special attention would be paid to promoting the position of the developing countries in international trade.

The plan to conclude the negotiations within four years failed. The closing date was postponed several times. In particular, the negotiations were held up for a long time by the lack of agreement between the EC and the US on reducing agricultural subsidies. Eventually, in November 1992, the Blair House Accord was concluded between the EC and the US, which included an undertaking to reduce subsidised cereal exports and also to guarantee a minimum level of market access for foreign suppliers of agricultural products. The agreement subsequently encountered much opposition in France: people there were not prepared to accept it without amendment, while the Americans were for a long time unwilling to re-negotiate what had been agreed. During 1993 the agricultural question therefore became more and more a matter between the French and the Americans. In the end, the Americans were after all prepared to make some adjustments to the Blair House Accord so that it would be acceptable to the French. This opened the way for an overall agreement between what had now been renamed the European Union (EU) and the US, followed by a final agreement on the whole Uruguay Round on 15 December 1993.

The end result of the Uruguay Round for the agricultural sector eventually comprised the following points:

- non-tariff barriers are to be converted to equivalent tariffs, i.e. tariffs having a protective effect equivalent to the non-tariff measures in question. In some cases this may lead to very high tariffs of several hundred per cent, e.g. rice in Japan, which was hitherto subject to a total import ban. The tariffs must be bound and subsequently reduced by an average of 36 per cent over a six-year period from 1995. This once again shows the GATT preference for tariffs rather than other types of trade restriction, because tariffs keep the market mechanism operating;
- in addition, by the end of the implementation period, foreign suppliers of agricul-

Figure 2.1 The Franco-American conflict over agriculture, as seen by a cartoonist in *The Economist*, 18 September 1993 [ref. p. 36]

tural products must have a minimum market share of 5 per cent of domestic consumption;

- export subsidies on seventeen agricultural products (including cereals, meat, dairy products) must within six years be cut by 36 per cent compared to the 1986–90 period. The volume of subsidised exports has to be cut by 21 per cent over the same period.

As regards another important aspect of the round, the services sector, significant results were achieved in that a framework of principles and rules for trade in services, the General Agreement on Trade in Services (GATS), was accepted, stipulating the basic obligations of the participating countries, such as most-favoured-nation treatment for foreign suppliers of services and, for some sectors, national treatment of foreign suppliers. No agreement was reached on a number of sub-sectors within the services sector, such as the audio-visual sector, telecommunications and maritime transport. Regarding the audio-visual sector, which concerns films, television programmes and the like, there was again conflict between the French and the

Box 2.3: The role of Peter Sutherland in the final phase of the Uruguay Round

Until late in the autumn of 1993 it was unclear whether the Uruguay Round could be successfully concluded by 15 December, the expiry date of the American president's authority to 'fast track' the outcome of the round through Congress.

The fact that the round was successful is certainly not thanks to the French, who demanded that the November 1992 Blair House Accord on agriculture be amended. The Americans regarded the whole Uruguay Round as so important that they eventually complied with this demand.

A significant role in the success of the round was played by the man who succeeded Arthur Dunkel in mid-1993 as Director General of the GATT: the Irishman Peter Sutherland. In the 12 June 1993 issue *The Economist*, which refers to him as King Peter, describes him as a man who combines his Irish charm with rugby-playing pugnacity and a barrister's sharpness. He always impressed the great importance of the Uruguay Round upon the main players, and was always totally clear about the need to conclude the round by 15 December 1993. Otherwise, the GATT would be dead on 16 December.

Americans. France feared that its 'cultural identity' would be impaired if French restrictions, such as those on the showing of American television programmes, had to be liberalised.

In the more traditional sphere of tariff reduction, the Uruguay Round also made further progress: tariffs on industrial products were to fall by an average of over one third. Another new feature is that concessions on this point were required – and obtained – from the developing countries, particularly in the category of Newly Industrialising Economies.

Where the Tokyo Round had failed to reach agreement on safeguards, the Uruguay Round now succeeded. The use of safeguards is subject to discipline by the application of time limits, requirements concerning examination prior to the application of measures and, in general, by the continued requirement concerning non-discrimination. This will eventually end grey-area measures such as the VERs. In this connection it was also agreed to dismantle the Multifibre Agreement over a ten-year period.

A new area in which agreement was reached was the protection of intellectual property rights. Patents were protected for twenty years and copyrights for fifty.

Another result of the Uruguay Round is that the GATT as an international organisation became the World Trade Organisation (WTO) in 1995. This means that there is at last a fully fledged international organisation in the sphere of international trade, with a Ministerial Conference as its supreme authority; there will be a General Council to deal with everyday business. One of the features of the new organisation will be a more binding procedure for settling disputes than that under the GATT (see also a subsequent section in this chapter).

Although, as we have seen, the Uruguay Round was not successful on every point, implementation of the agreements reached is nevertheless expected to give a substantial boost to the world economy. Thus, a joint study by the World Bank and the OECD expects a possible increase in global annual income of over $200 billion.[7] It is as yet difficult to say to what extent developing countries will also benefit: positive measures such as liberalisation in the tropical products sphere are offset by intellectual property protection measures which could be detrimental to developing countries. The measures in the agricultural sector, which are expected to lead to an increase in world market prices by cutting export subsidies, will have contrasting short- and long-term effects. In the short term the developing countries which import food will be worse off; in the longer term, they may benefit as their own food production will be stimulated by higher prices.

2.7 Unfair foreign trade practices: GATT/WTO rules on national complaints procedures

As we have already seen, an important function of the GATT is to formulate rules covering the way countries conduct their trade policy. One aspect of this merits separate mention, namely the rules governing the procedures for handling complaints of unfair foreign trade practices, particularly dumping and the subsidising of foreign products. Dumping means that a private exporter offers his product abroad at a price below the 'normal' value in the exporting country, usually the domestic market price in that country. Subsidies to foreign competitors are subsidies on production or exportation of goods granted by foreign governments, leading directly or indirectly to growth in exports of the products in question. As an international agreement, the GATT makes provision, in Article VI, for the introduction of anti-dumping duties or, in the case of subsidies, countervailing duties in the importing country if material injury is caused or is threatened to be caused to an established domestic industry, or if the establishment of such an industry is materially retarded.

The anti-dumping and anti-subsidy procedures are generally initiated by the domestic industry in the importing country which considers itself the injured party and therefore complains to the national government about any foreign competitor suspected of unfair trade practices.

As already stated, the regulatory role of the GATT is expressed in Article VI of the General Agreement. This article is in Part II of the treaty, which means that it applies only in so far as it is not contrary to existing national legislation. The evocative expression 'grandfather clause' is used here: the 'grandfather', someone with existing rights, is a metaphor for previous national legislation. In order to circumvent this problem, there has been consultation on this issue in the course of the GATT's

---

[7] I. Goldin *et al.*, *Trade Liberalization: Global Economic Implications*, OECD, Paris and World Bank, Washington DC, 1993.

Figure 2.2   Article from *The Economist*, 4 April 1992 [ref. p. 42]

Get your fax right

PROTECTIONIST ploys are often used to coddle mature industries in decline, not to protect firms in markets about to disappear altogether. But the European Community seems to be trying to do just this.

Last October the European Commission imposed provisional duties of up to 55% on imports of Japanese thermal fax-paper. The move was prompted by a complaint from Arjo Wiggins Appleton, an Anglo-French paper company, that Japanese producers were depressing prices by dumping fax paper in the British market. On March 16th the commission announced that the duties will continue until further notice.

The commission's investigation confirmed that prices of fax paper were higher in Japan than in Europe. This, it claimed, meant that Japanese producers were guilty of dumping. That, at best, is debatable. Almost every product is more expensive in Japan than in Europe.

But more puzzling is the commission's claim that, without dumping duties, European companies (ie, Arjo Wiggins Appleton) might have to stop making fax paper. "Sustaining over the long term a viable industry in this sector," it concluded, out-weighed the cost to consumers of more expensive fax paper.

The trouble with this reasoning is that there is no long-term future for thermal fax-paper. Ask a local office supplier for "fax paper" five years from now and you will probably be greeted with a blank look. The fax machines now sitting in most of Europe's offices use thermal paper. But the average life of a fax machine is only five years, and most new models available today, thanks to advances in printer technology, use ordinary paper, just as photocopiers do. Cheaper machines still require thermal paper, but the price of plain-paper models is dropping fast.

Thermal paper, of which fax paper is simply one variety, will continue to be used in other applications, such as labels and tickets, but the EC's duties do not cover those products. So the EC's anti-dumping duty looks decidedly un-long-term. The only beneficiaries will be Arjo Wiggins Appleton's shareholders, for a while.

existence. In the case of the anti-dumping procedures this was done in the Kennedy Round and subsequent rounds, which led to the establishment of codes of conduct. Countries signing this Anti-Dumping Code lose the option of invoking the grandfather clause. Such a code for national procedures concerning countervailing duties was established for the first time in the Tokyo Round, as already mentioned in the section on that subject.

The rules on anti-dumping and anti-subsidy procedures have not always succeeded in preventing domestic industries competing with imports from abusing these procedures for protectionist purposes, and the impression is growing that this has been happening more frequently as time goes by. Figure 2.2 presents a striking example of abuse of the anti-dumping procedure.

One reason for the abuse of the anti-dumping procedure is the asymmetry between the position of the complainant and the accused, in that it costs the complainant little to submit a complaint, while the accused faces very high costs, mainly on account of the need to bring in expensive legal advisers.

The fact that anti-dumping and anti-subsidy procedures are not always used correctly led to consultations on tighter rules in the Uruguay Round. As far as anti-dumping procedures are concerned, this resulted in more stringent requirements for ascertaining the causal connection between dumping and injury to the domestic industry. The accused exporters were also given procedural guarantees whereby they could defend themselves, and the duration of anti-dumping duties was restricted.

As regards subsidies and countervailing duties, a significant result of the Uruguay Round was that specific subsidies were divided into three categories. This covers all government financial contributions which have the object or effect of benefiting one company or sector. The three types of subsidy are symbolised by the colours of a set of traffic lights. The first category contains prohibited, or red, subsidies, which includes export subsidies. The second is for subsidies which are not immune to countervailing measures, or orange subsidies. This type of subsidy is regarded as automatically causing serious damage to other countries if the value of the subsidy represents more than 5 per cent of the price. In this case the burden of proof is reversed and no longer rests with the importing country. Finally, there is the category of immune or green subsidies. Countervailing duties may not be imposed on products supported by these subsidies. This category includes subsidies for industrial research.

A change in both the anti-dumping and the anti-subsidy rules is that they no longer apply only to countries which have signed the relevant codes of conduct, but to all members of the new World Trade Organisation.

2.8 Dispute settlement

Another important aspect of the GATT/WTO's activities is dispute settlement: this concerns mainly disputes in which the country considering itself the injured party pleads that the trade policy of the accused country is resulting in 'nullification or impairment' of concessions previously granted under the GATT. In response, the injured party may also withdraw trade concessions worth an equivalent amount, in accordance with the principle of reciprocity. In the first instance, an attempt will be made to settle this type of dispute by persuading the countries concerned to try consultation and reconciliation. If that fails, then a panel of independent experts may be brought in. If the decision of the experts is unanimously accepted by the Council of Representatives, the injured country is entitled to take counter-measures. The problem is that the required unanimity is often blocked by the accused country: that is one reason why, in the Uruguay Round, ways of improving the dispute settlement procedure were sought. The new World Trade Organisation will in fact have a more stringent procedure in that there will be strict time limits for each stage in the procedure and the system will be virtually automatic. This means that a panel report is automatically accepted within a specified period unless there is a consensus in favour of rejection. This eliminates the accused party's right of veto. Another amendment concerns the possibility of tackling measures taken unilaterally by individual countries.

2.9 New areas of focus for the GATT/WTO

Eastern Europe

The recent upheavals in Eastern Europe also had consequences for the GATT. Previously, relations between the GATT and the planned economies of Eastern Europe were either difficult or totally non-existent.

Although the Soviet Union was initially involved in the consultations on the post-war institutional framework as regards international trade policy, in the end it did not join the GATT. Czechoslovakia was the only East European country to participate in the GATT right from the start. For other countries, an important reason for not joining was the fear that, in a world with unequal levels of development, the GATT principle of non-discrimination would work to the advantage of the more developed countries. Also, the idea of a multilateral trade system was difficult to reconcile with the system of central planning in force at the time, in which bilateral trade agreements with other countries were the usual way of conducting international trade (see also Chapter 7).

There are bound to be problems in incorporating into the system countries with an economic system based on central planning. This is most obvious if we look again at the basic principles of the GATT, stated at the beginning of this chapter: non-discrimination, reciprocity and emphasis on import tariffs as the only permitted trade policy instrument. The problem is concentrated on the tariff instrument which, according to the GATT philosophy, is preferable because it influences trade without disabling the market mechanism. In centrally planned economies, however, tariffs have no meaning as instruments that influence trade indirectly because decisions on trade are taken directly by the planning authorities. As a result, the basic GATT principle of non-discrimination in the sense of application of the same tariffs to all trading partners is meaningless. Reciprocity in the form of an exchange of equivalent tariff concessions cannot be applied either. This explains why, in the case of Poland and Romania, which joined the GATT in 1967 and 1971 respectively, after reassessing the advantages and disadvantages of participation, different kinds of requirement were imposed in order to guarantee reciprocity, namely quantitative obligations concerning imports from the GATT countries. In the case of Hungary, which joined in 1973, such requirements were not imposed because it was believed that Hungary had already reformed its economic system sufficiently for the 'normal' GATT treatment to be applied.

The significance of the participation of the East European planned economies in the GATT was limited, partly because in the West – and especially in the EC –

quantitative restrictions on imports from these countries remained in force. These restrictions applying specifically to the planned economies were not lifted until after the turmoil of 1989 (see Chapter 7).

Following the upheavals and the switch to market-economy principles, the East European countries wanted the special requirements formerly imposed on them to be lifted. Apart from the quantitative obligations regarding imports from GATT countries, already mentioned above, there were special safeguards concerning imports from Eastern Europe in addition to those normally applicable to GATT countries.

Environment questions

The increasing interest in problems concerning the natural environment also had repercussions on trade policy. There are various areas in which the two subjects overlap. Particularly relevant to this chapter on the GATT/WTO are questions concerning the extent to which trade policy can be used as an instrument of environmental policy and to what extent trade policy measures can be used to compensate for the effects of environmental measures on the competitive position of a country. In the case of the first question, the GATT principle of national treatment is important: a country can prohibit the sale of foreign products on environmental grounds only if the same rules apply to home-produced goods. Thus, in 1982, in a GATT disputes procedure in which Canada contested the American ban on imports of Canadian tuna and tuna-based products, Canada won the case because there had been no action on tuna caught by American fishermen.

The question of the use of trade policy instruments to compensate for the effects of environmental measures on the competitive position is rather more complex. Let us consider the example of a country which takes the lead in applying strict environmental standards at home in order to combat production which pollutes the environment. On the question of whether that country should be able to use trade policy measures to compensate for the impairment of its competitive position, we should mention a report by the GATT secretariat which strongly warns against so doing.[8] For example, it states that it is natural for developed countries to pursue a stricter environment policy than developing countries. Another point is that, in principle, all differences in government policy between countries influence the competitive position, so that these differences can also form part of the basis for international trade. Also, although a stricter environment policy can be a disadvantage in the short term, there may be advantages for the competitive position in the longer term because other countries have to follow suit sooner or later. Thus, there could be a J-curve effect by analogy with the curve familiar from the literature showing the link between depreciation of a currency and the developments in the country's balance of payments over a period of time. There is a deterioration in the short term, followed by an improvement which only emerges later.

---

[8] GATT Secretariat, 'Trade and the environment' in *International Trade in 90/91*, Vol. I, Geneva, 1992, pp. 19–43.

2.10 The European Union and the GATT/WTO

Although countries belonging to the European Union were separate GATT contracting parties and are separate WTO members, they act jointly in their trade policy in relation to third countries (see also Chapter 6). For the GATT rounds of negotiations this has meant that the European Commission negotiates on behalf of the European Union countries. It is sometimes claimed that the joint operation of the EU countries in the GATT negotiations has delayed progress: all EU Member States first have to agree on their joint position, which leaves little scope for negotiating with other countries. The laborious decision-making within the EC did in fact appear to delay the Uruguay Round, especially in the crucial negotiations on trade in agricultural products.

One factor in the EU's decision-making is that the various member states have different preferences as regards the choice between further trade liberalisation and the maintenance of existing protection measures. This may be to do with different ideologies, but also with different national interests. Thus, countries with a very open economy, in the sense that international trade makes a very substantial contribution to total economic activity, have more interest in keeping international markets open than countries for which international trade is less important. Another significant tendency here is that trade within the EU is increasing in relation to external trade by the EU countries. This may result in less importance being attached to global trade liberalisation under the GATT. This would be a bad thing not only for those EU countries for which a significant proportion of their trade is still with non-EU members, but probably also for the EU as a whole. Even a large bloc like the EU needs external competition in order to 'stay alert' and continue striving for maximum efficiency of production. Take the car sector, for instance, where Japanese competition, in particular, is forcing the European car industry to remain competitive.

2.11 Free trade: theory *versus* practice

The question which has already arisen several times in this chapter is this: if free trade is actually so beneficial, why is there so much resistance to it in practice? Ultimately it is because the benefits and costs are shared in different ways between the different groups in society, and these groups try to defend their interests by influencing trade policy decisions. This brings us to the 'political economy' of the choice between free trade and protection. An industry in danger of losing its protection, such as agriculture in the Uruguay Round, has a definite interest in preserving it. Moreover, in the national and – in the case of the EU – European context, agriculture has a very well-organised lobby, sometimes known as the Green Front.

More generally, groups with an interest in protection are often small, strongly-motivated groups, set against the relatively minor and/or more diffuse interests of those parties opposed to protection. This makes it difficult for the opponents to organise an anti-protection lobby and raise enough money for a lobby campaign.

Opponents of protection are primarily consumers who object to the way in which protection raises prices. Second, there are exporters who may be impeded in various ways by protection in their own country. Since other countries take counter-measures, protection can be detrimental to their access to foreign markets. Another effect operates via the exchange rate: protection will lead to an appreciation of the country's currency, damaging the exporters' competitive position. Another category of persons opposed to protection consists of domestic producers who use the protected imports as components or semi-manufactures in their production processes.

Another factor in the conflict is that the advantages of protection are evident in the short term, as are the disadvantages of eliminating it – namely the destruction of businesses which can no longer compete – while the advantages of liberalisation often take longer to become apparent and are much harder to detect.

Bibliography

Anderson, K. and Blackhurst, R. (eds.), *The Greening of World Trade Issues*, New York, 1992.

Bhagwati, J., *Protectionism*, Cambridge (Mass.) and London, 1988.

Bhagwati, J., *The World Trading System at Risk*, New York, 1991.

Dam, K. W., *The GATT: Law and International Economic Organization*, Chicago and London, 1970.

GATT, *The Tokyo Round of Multilateral Trade Negotiations; Report by the Director-General*, Geneva, 1979.

Gardner, R. N., *Sterling–Dollar Diplomacy in Current Perspective: The Origins and the Prospects of Our International Economic Order*, New York, 1980.

Goldin I., *et al.*, *Trade Liberalization: Global Economic Implications*, Paris and Washington DC, 1993.

Greenaway, D., *International Trade Policy: From Tariffs to the New Protectionism*, London and Basingstoke, 1983.

Greenaway, D. and Hindley, B., *What Britain Pays for Voluntary Export Restraints*, Thames Essay No 43, London, 1985, p. 59.

Krauss, M. B., *The New Protectionism: The Welfare State and International Trade*, New York, 1978.

Preeg, E. H., *Traders and Diplomats: An Analysis of the Kennedy Round of Negotiations under the General Agreement on Tariffs and Trade*, Washington DC, 1970.

World Bank, *World Development Report 1987*, in particular Part II on the subject of 'Industrialization and Foreign Trade', New York, 1987.

Winham, G. R., *International Trade and the Tokyo Round Negotiation*, Princeton, 1986.

GATT/WTO publications

FOCUS, WTO Newsletter. Published ten times a year with news of WTO activities.

GATT Activities 19 . . . [reporting year]. Annual publication on the various activities of the GATT Secretariat.

International Trade in . . . / . . . [reporting years]. Annual publication with figures and analytical surveys of world trade developments.

Basic Instruments and Selected Documents. Annual publication on important decisions, recommendations and reports approved by the contracting parties in the year in question.

Address

World Trade Organisation
Centre William Rappard
154 Rue de Lausanne
1211 Geneva 21
Switzerland

3 United Nations organisations and arrangements

3.1 Introduction

This chapter will consider the role of the United Nations in international trade and trade policy. We begin with the most important organ, which is particularly concerned with questions relating to the position of developing countries in international trade. This is followed by a review of the importance of the regional economic commissions, particularly for the international trade of the regions in question. Next we shall discuss the involvement of the United Nations in the activities of transnational corporations. Finally, we consider the role of the United Nations in environmental questions, particularly as regards the consequences for international trade.

3.2 The UN Conference on Trade and Development (UNCTAD)

During the 1950s and 1960s, developing countries became increasingly dissatisfied with their position in the world economy. There were a whole range of reasons for this, but only those relating to international trade and trade policy will be dealt with here. A distinction can be made between problems concerning trade in commodities and those relating to trade in manufactures.

As regards commodities, on which developing countries are traditionally dependent for a large proportion of their export earnings, the two essential problems are price instability and the long-term trend in the relative price of commodities vis-à-vis industrial products. In general, commodity prices are subject to greater fluctuations than prices of industrial products. Fluctuations in commodity prices can lead to variations in the export earnings of developing countries, heavily dependent on these products. The developing countries consider that this is detrimental to their prospects for economic development.

As regards the long-term trend in the relative price of commodities, the developing countries have more than once expressed the opinion that the terms of trade are turning against them: i.e., the prices of their export products are not rising as fast as the prices of their imports. Chapter 5 will deal with empirical and theoretical aspects of the question of the terms of trade of developing countries.

Where international trade in industrial products is concerned, a major grievance of the developing countries was that the GATT trade liberalisation negotiations mainly yielded favourable results for the export products of industrial countries, but achieved much less for products important to developing countries' exports. They also refer to the phenomenon of 'tariff escalation', which means that tariffs on imports of commodities into industrial countries are low or totally non-existent, but become ever higher on items at further stages of the production process which use the commodities in their manufacture. This results in a high 'effective rate of protection', i.e. a much higher value added is possible in the production process of the industrial countries than would be possible without tariff escalation. This works against the processing of commodities in the developing countries.

Another objection directed at the GATT system by developing countries is that non-discrimination is a central element, while the developing countries consider that they ought to be given a preferential position in the trade policy of industrial countries because they are less developed. This is in fact a variant of the infant-industry argument which is generally used to justify protection of a nation's own industry, but in this case is used to secure preferential treatment in export markets.

These objections to the prevailing world trade system were among the reasons why the developing countries wanted to set up an international organisation concentrating on their interests. As a result of the first plenary session of the United Nations Conference on Trade and Development (UNCTAD) in Geneva in 1964, this aim was realised by the establishment of UNCTAD as a permanent international organisation. The Trade and Development Board was the permanent policy-making body with committees under it for the various types of problem with which UNCTAD is concerned. A permanent secretariat was also set up, headed by a Secretary General. This post was first held by Raul Prebisch, who together with Hans Singer was responsible for the above-mentioned thesis of the systematic deterioration in the terms of trade for the developing countries. After the first conference in 1964, plenary sessions of the UNCTAD conferences took place at intervals of three to four years.

For a proper understanding of UNCTAD as an international organisation, it is important to realise that UNCTAD itself does not have any executive powers in the policy spheres with which it is concerned. UNCTAD conference resolutions constitute recommendations to the United Nations General Assembly, which UNCTAD comes under. Here UNCTAD differs from specialised agencies within the UN family, such as the International Monetary Fund, the FAO (Food and Agriculture Organisation) and the ILO (International Labour Organisation), which do have their own executive functions.

The Group of 77 also originally manifested itself at the first UNCTAD conference: this was a pressure group formed by the developing countries to bring about changes in the existing international economic order. This group, which now has far more than seventy-seven members, later also tackled problems facing developing countries on other fronts.

If we go on to consider what UNCTAD has achieved since it was set up, there is little of substance to record on the first UNCTAD conference. The developing countries tended to use the 'voting machine' to get resolutions passed on the basis of their numerical majority against the will of the Western countries. As a result, the resolutions had no practical consequences in the form of policy changes in the Western world. The second UNCTAD conference in New Delhi in 1968 therefore went for a more consensus-based approach rather than confrontation. An important practical result of UNCTAD II was the creation of the Generalised System of Preferences (GSP), whereby OECD countries apply preferential tariffs on a non-reciprocal basis to imports of primarily manufactures and semi-manufactures from developing countries, in order to raise export earnings in those countries and thus stimulate the growth of their industry. The aforementioned infant industry argument is put forward here in favour of preferential treatment.

In general, industrial products which come under the system are imported free of duty into OECD countries. Contrary to what the name Generalised System of Preferences might indicate, the various OECD countries or blocs such as the EC interpret differently the idea of preferential treatment of imports from developing countries. The EC GSP was the first to be introduced on 1 July 1971, followed by systems in most other industrial countries by the end of 1972. Canada and the US completed the series with the implementation of their GSP, in 1974 and 1976 respectively.

The GSP was made possible by an addition to the GATT in 1965 (Part IV), in which developing countries are largely exempt from the principles of non-discrimination and reciprocity. On that basis, for the first period of the GSP from 1971 to 1980 the GATT contracting parties introduced a waiver, granting an exception to the most-favoured-nation clause. Later, in connection with the extension of the GSP, agreement was reached in the Tokyo Round on an enabling clause which, apart from extending the GSP, also permitted its restriction in the case of developing countries which have already made substantial progress in their development process and have thus achieved 'graduation'. This means that they should, to a greater extent, be treated in accordance with the general GATT rules.

From this we see that UNCTAD and the GATT/WTO are both concerned with the trade policy aspects of development. The principal difference is that UNCTAD deals only with the interests of the developing countries and endeavours to secure preferential treatment for those countries, while the GATT/WTO has the broader task of considering the interests of all countries involved. Another important difference is that between the status of the GATT trade policy agreements and an UNCTAD agreement on the GSP, for example. The GATT agreements on trade policy, resulting from the various rounds of negotiations, constitute binding contractual obligations on the countries concerned. The GSP is not a mutually binding contract between Western countries and developing countries, but a unilateral decision by the Western countries which can thus also be unilaterally amended or even withdrawn. This means that the developing countries are in the last instance dependent on the good will of the industrial countries as regards their preferential treatment in terms of trade policy.

Although the introduction of the GSP was, in principle, an important step towards stimulating the exports of developing countries, its actual significance should not be over-estimated. Thus, sectors where developing countries traditionally perform well, such as textiles and the leather industry, are totally excluded or subject to restricted preferences. There are also all kinds of restrictions on the other product categories, such as in the case of the EC GSP: tariff quotas which limit the total value of imports eligible for preferential treatment per product, ceilings per exporting developing country and restrictions per importing EC country.

While the creation of the GSP was UNCTAD's principal achievement in the 1960s and early 1970s, as far as UNCTAD was concerned the rest of the 1970s were given over to consultations on international commodity arrangements. The climate for this was in fact created by the first oil crisis in 1973, which showed that, by joint action within OPEC, a group of developing countries were able to secure a substantial increase in the price of their export product, in this case oil (for more on OPEC, see Chapter 5). Oil-importing industrial countries feared that similar producer cartels would also operate for other products. This made them willing to conduct UNCTAD consultations on commodities and other matters relevant to developing countries. The umbrella formula used in this connection is that of the New International Economic Order (NIEO). The existing international economic order needed to be amended in a number of respects to create an order which would be fairer to the developing countries. The new order was established by the adoption of the Declaration and Programme of Action on the Establishment of a New International Economic Order by the United Nations General Assembly in May 1974. As well as referring to commodities, this stressed the following aims:

- improvement of the GSP;
- improved access to markets in developed countries for exports from developing countries;
- reform of the international monetary system;
- cancellation or restructuring of developing countries' debts;
- establishment of a code of conduct for the transfer of technology to developing countries;
- regulation of the activities of multinational corporations.

As far as commodities are concerned, it was declared that an Integrated Programme for Commodities was required. This idea had already been launched in the 1960s by the UNCTAD Secretariat, but came to nothing because of the opposition by industrial countries. The Integrated Programme for Commodities is often seen as the *pièce de résistance* of the NIEO. The fourth UNCTAD conference in Nairobi in 1976 approved the details of the Integrated Programme for Commodities, prepared by the secretariat. This included in particular the establishment of a system of international buffer stocks of a large number of commodities, intended to stabilise the prices of the commodities concerned by the buffer stock authority selling stocks when prices were too high or buying stocks when prices were too low. The buffer stocks were to be financed by a Common Fund. The idea behind this is that joint financing is cheaper if the movements in the prices of the various commodities are not fully synchronised. For example, if the price of certain commodities is too high, so that

---

Box 3.1: The fate of the Common Fund

Amsterdam became the home of the Common Fund when it was eventually launched in 1989. An important reason for choosing Amsterdam was undoubtedly that the Netherlands generally welcomed the idea of setting up commodity agreements between producer and consumer countries. Among the group of industrial nations, it was one of those most receptive to the demands of the developing countries to establish a New International Economic Order, including the desire for a Common Fund to finance a series of commodity agreements. However, when it was eventually established, the fund was 'trimmed down', and did not handle the joint financing of a number of commodity agreements – originally defined as its main task – because there were insufficient commodity agreements in operation. The 'second window' of the fund did operate, however: this aimed to finance projects in the sphere of diversification, marketing and product improvement. Overall, however, the fund has insufficient resources, and some countries, including Switzerland and Canada, have already resigned their membership.

---

resources become available as a result of sales of those commodities, the money could be used to buy commodities currently under-priced (for a more detailed explanation of the operation of buffer stocks, see Chapter 5). The programme would comprise eighteen core commodities. Apart from the jointly financed buffer stocks, the integrated programme also included some other elements such as the improvement of the compensatory financing scheme for countries whose earnings from commodity exports are declining, and the promotion of industrial processing of commodities by the developing countries.

Problems arose in the implementation of the integrated programme for commodities which, after the negotiations had dragged on for years, eventually led to the whole undertaking becoming bogged down. One of the problems in the negotiations was whether the Common Fund should take over a series of individual commodity agreements already concluded – the position adopted by the industrial countries – or whether the Common Fund should stimulate the conclusion of agreements or even be used to stabilise markets for which no agreement had been reached, which was the view of the developing countries. In the end, the industrial countries got their way on this. However, the climate has now altered so much that the whole idea of the Integrated Programme for Commodities has in fact been superseded. There are various factors at work here. In general, belief in the scope for government intervention in market processes has now declined greatly. More specifically, as regards the Integrated Programme for Commodities, the long periods of recession when commodity prices are low right across the board indicate that the basic idea of the programme, utilising differential price movements between individual commodities, does not always apply. Moreover, the frightening image of the OPEC cartel is fading because it does not appear capable of dictating oil prices in the long term (for more about this see Chapter 5). Another category of problems concerns the operation of individual commodity agreements. These problems are also relevant to a joint approach; they too will be discussed in Chapter 5.

Another subject which is relevant to this book and which has always concerned UNCTAD is economic integration between developing countries. The idea here is that developing countries will become less dependent on their trade with industrial countries via mutual trade liberalisation. Raul Prebisch, mentioned earlier, was a prominent supporter of this idea, especially in his previous capacity as Secretary General of the regional economic commission for Latin America (see also the next section).

As regards the importance of UNCTAD in the present world economy, we are bound to state that the organisation has been sidelined. We have already seen how the plan for an Integrated Programme for Commodities largely failed. The broader concept of creating a New International Economic Order met the same fate. Apart from the changed attitude towards the desirability of interfering with market forces, the fact that, as a developing countries pressure group, the Group of 77 is becoming less and less homogeneous as time goes by is also an important factor. Thus, there are many developing countries nowadays that are no longer dependent on commodity exports. A number, particularly the newly industrialising nations, have fought their way out of that position and have now become exporters of industrial products on a substantial scale. Thus, this group of countries is no longer necessarily interested in maximum prices for commodities. Precisely the opposite is true in the case of commodities which they use as inputs in their industrial production processes.

Another trend which should be mentioned here is that people in developing countries are focusing less on international factors as the reason why the development process has not got off the ground, and now realise the defects in their own domestic policy.

3.3 The United Nations regional economic commissions

In the belief that certain economic problems can be better tackled on a regional scale, the United Nations Economic and Social Council (ECOSOC) decided to set up regional economic commissions. In 1947 the Economic Commission for Europe (ECE) was founded with its headquarters in Geneva, and the Economic Commission for Asia and the Far East (ECAFE) was set up in Bangkok. In 1974 the latter commission was renamed the Economic and Social Commission for Asia and the Pacific (ESCAP). The Economic Commission for Latin America (ECLA) was founded in 1948, with its headquarters in Santiago, Chile. The Commission was expanded in 1983 to include the Caribbean region: since then it has been known as the Economic Commission for Latin America and the Caribbean (ECLAC). After increasing numbers of African countries achieved independence, the Economic Commission for Africa (ECA) was set up in 1958 with its headquarters in Addis Ababa. The newest regional commission is the Economic Commission for Western Asia (ECWA) set up in 1973, initially in Beirut but eventually ending up in Baghdad after various moves.

Membership of the regional economic commissions is not confined to countries in the region. Thus, industrial countries – including the United States and the United Kingdom – are members of ECLAC and ESCAP.

The regional economic commissions have varying objectives for less developed regions and for Europe. The first commissions mentioned concentrate heavily on the joint economic and social development of the region, while in Europe there is no joint development problem. In the less developed regions the regional economic commissions play an important role in advising governments on development planning and training government officials.

An objective which does apply to all commissions is the most important one from this book's point of view: that of promoting intra-regional trade. In Latin America the ECLA played a major role in the establishment of the Latin American Free Trade Association (LAFTA) and the Central American Common Market (CACM). In Africa, the ECA studied the feasibility of creating an African common market, but nothing concrete came of it. Economic integration between developing countries will be discussed in more detail in Chapter 6.

The ECE was also concerned with international trade in Europe, particularly between the Western market economies and the centrally planned economies of Eastern Europe. For a long time this was the only international forum where European countries could discuss their trade problems. And for a long time, particularly in the 1950s and 1960s, none of the East European countries (except one or two) belonged to the GATT. One specific activity of the ECE was the development of industrial standards, the most familiar to the general public being the standard for assessing petrol consumption by cars.

A new issue which is to concern the regional commissions is that of energy and environmental policy. The ECE has taken the lead in energy policy with the Energy Efficiency 2000 Project (EE 2000), launched in 1991. The purpose of this is to promote trade and co-operation in energy-saving, environment-friendly technology, particularly between the former planned economies and the market economies. This project is to be copied by the other regional economic commissions, eventually leading to a Global Energy Efficiency 21 Project (GEE 21).

Finally, an activity of the United Nations regional commissions, and especially their secretariats, which ought to be mentioned is the publication of information on economic trends in the regions concerned.

3.4 The United Nations and transnational corporations

During the period following World War II, multinational or transnational corporations became an increasingly common phenomenon. These are corporations which have branches in several countries where some of their activities take place. The reason for establishing branches elsewhere may vary: it may be in order to obtain primary products, but also to utilise lower production costs or serve local markets. This book is particularly interested in how multinationals affect international trade and trade policy and the activities of international organisations in that field. In this connection, the principal effect of the increasing scale of operations of multinationals is that an ever higher proportion of international trade is represented by intra-firm trade, and thus no longer takes place via markets. One result of this is that the impact of trade policy measures is not the same as for market transactions. Thus with intra-firm trade, an import tariff need not lead to a higher domestic price for the product concerned, because the exporting division of the firm can reduce its selling price and thus cut the amount which the multinational has to pay in import duties. More generally, multinationals can adjust their internal supply prices, the transfer prices, in an attempt to keep their tax bills to the minimum by reducing taxable amounts in countries with high tax rates and doing the opposite in countries where rates are low. This behaviour where taxes are concerned is an example of a more general phenomenon whereby multinationals attempt to evade the policy of the national authorities in countries where they are established.

Another aspect of the multinationals which is relevant in the light of international trade policy concerns the services sector. As already stated in the chapter on the GATT/WTO, in the account of the Uruguay Round, there is often a direct connection between international trade and local investment in the services sector. The whole of the (potential) host country's government policy on this is involved here, and not just trade policy as in the case of international trade in goods.

The aspects mentioned here are part of the reason why international organisations, including the United Nations, will be looking at the question of multinationals. A point which should be made is that the attitude to multinationals has changed greatly over the years from somewhat hostile in the 1960s and 1970s to moderately positive in the latter half of the 1980s. The negative view in the earlier period was due mainly to the scandals concerning political meddling by multinationals in host countries, often in the developing country category, the best known being the case of the International Telephone & Telegraph Company (ITT) in Chile. In the early 1970s this American company was very actively involved in attempts to bring down the Marxist President of Chile, Salvador Allende, because of fears that the company's assets in Chile would be nationalised by the Allende government.

One reason for the change of attitude among developing countries in the 1980s was the debt crisis at the beginning of this period, when many developing countries had to contend with foreign exchange shortages. One way of reducing these deficits without creating new external debts was to attract investment by multinationals. The role of the multinationals as sources of technology was also re-evaluated.

In 1974 the United Nations' ECOSOC set up the intergovernmental Commission on Transnational Corporations, which was to take a close interest in questions relating to multinationals, its primary aim being to establish a code of conduct for such organisations.[2] After years of consultations a draft United Nations Code of Conduct on Transnational Corporations was produced in 1988, laying down rules for the conduct of multinationals. These rules concerned both government policy on multinationals

---

[2] The United Nations consistently refers to 'transnational' and not multinational corporations. However, the distinction is not sufficiently important for us to worry about it here. The two terms are therefore used interchangeably in this book.

and rules for the conduct of the multinationals themselves. The latter stipulated that the internal transfer prices used should be based on market prices for the goods in question (the arm's length principle). Application of this principle was intended to prevent multinationals from manipulating these prices to their own advantage but to the detriment of the national governments concerned.

Another important element of the draft code of conduct concerned the principle of the treatment of multinationals by (potential) host countries. The stated principle is one of 'fair and equitable treatment': this does not go so far as the principle of national treatment, whereby domestic companies and foreign investors must be treated equally. The latter principle does apply to the treatment of foreign corporations in the OECD-countries, as we shall see in Chapter 4. The much vaguer compromise formula of the UN draft code reveals the influence of developing countries, which wish to preserve the option of restricting the activities of foreign investors in certain cases, e.g. in sectors which they consider of crucial importance to their economic development, and in so doing to deviate from the principle of equal treatment.

So far the code of conduct has still not got beyond the draft stage. This is undoubtedly because of the aforementioned change in the attitude towards multinational corporations, which has reduced the apparent need for a code imposing all kinds of restrictions on multinationals.

Another UN body which ought to be mentioned here is the United Nations Centre on Transnational Corporations (UNCTC). This centre was established in 1975 to support the work of the Commission on Transnational Corporations which had been set up the previous year. Apart from offering training courses for government officials from developing countries, with the aim of improving the negotiating positions of those countries vis-à-vis multinationals, this centre also carries out research on multinational corporations, leading to highly informative and detailed publications.

3.5 The United Nations and environmental questions

Like other international organisations, the United Nations family is increasingly concerned with the environment. This is generally due to the growing realisation of the seriousness of environmental questions, but also more particularly to the international character of environmental pollution, indicating the need for an international approach.

Within the UN family, the United Nations Environmental Program (UNEP) has a central position in the environmental sphere. This body was set up in 1973 as a result of a decision by the General Assembly which in turn resulted from a recommendation by the UN Conference on the Environment, held in Stockholm in 1972. One of the aims of the UNEP is to promote international co-operation on the environment and recommend a policy for that purpose, as well as continuing to monitor the global environmental situation and bringing any problems to the attention of the governments concerned.

In 1987 the UNEP governing body adopted the report of the World Commission on Environment and Development (WCED) as a guide for future UNEP activities. This report is better known as the Brundtland report, named after the Norwegian chair of the Commission, which was set up at the time by the UN General Assembly for the purpose of examining the relationship between environmental questions and the problem of economic development.

An important contribution made by the Brundtland commission in its report *Our Common Future* was the coining of the term 'sustainable development', a concept which would constantly recur in subsequent international talks. According to the Brundtland Commission, sustainable development means meeting the needs of the present generation without endangering the satisfaction of the needs of future generations. In contrast, for instance, to the report in the early 1970s from the Club of Rome (an international organisation of individuals including industrialists and economists), it does not think in terms of a trade-off between the environment and economic development. Economic growth is considered necessary in order to solve the environment problem. In developing countries, the environment problem is seen primarily as a question of poverty.

As a result of a recommendation in the Brundtland report, the UN Conference on Environment and Development (UNCED), also known as the Earth Summit, was held in Rio de Janeiro in the summer of 1992. The conference led to:

- the Rio Declaration on environment and development, setting out the principles for environmental policy;
- Agenda 21, laying down a comprehensive action programme for sustainable development for the twenty-first century;
- a declaration on forests;
- two treaties: one on climatic change and one on biodiversity.

Although the above list might perhaps suggest that comprehensive decisions were taken, the UNCED should be seen more as an intermediate step in the process of making decisions on the environment and development. For instance, the conference did not settle the financing of Agenda 21 or the two treaties mentioned above.

Since this book is concerned primarily with the effects of the various international organisations and institutions on international trade, this section will conclude by outlining some of the UN-related arrangements which have had a specific impact on international trade. First we should mention the UN Convention on International Trade in Endangered Species of Wild Fauna and Flora (CITES). This convention imposes restrictions on international trade in such species: it was concluded in 1973.

Second, there was the Protocol of Montreal, dated 1987, which came about partly thanks to the efforts of the UNEP. The intention was to cut consumption of chlorofluorocarbons (CFCs) and thus help to protect the ozone layer. Imports of CFCs from non-participating countries were prohibited from 1 January 1991, and from 1 January 1993 imports of a number of products containing CFCs were prohibited from those countries.

Finally, the Basle Convention on the Control of Transboundary Movements of Hazardous Wastes and their Disposal, concluded in 1989, was also important.

Participating countries undertake to prohibit imports and exports of the substances concerned from/to non-participating countries.

Bibliography

Arntzen, J., Hemmer, I. and Kuik, O. (eds), *International Trade and Sustainable Development*, Amsterdam, 1992.

Bhagwati, J. N. (ed.), *The New International Economic Order: The North–South Debate*, Cambridge (Mass.), 1977.

Richards, J. H., *International Economic Institutions*, London, 1970, especially Chapter 1.

World Bank, 'Development and the Environment' in *World Development Report 1992*, New York, 1992.

Publications

UNITED NATIONS, GENERAL

Everyone's United Nations: Handbook of the Work of the United Nations, New York, 1986.

Basic Facts about the United Nations, New York, 1990.

The UN Chronicle. Quarterly journal with information on recent developments concerning the whole field of UN activities.

UNCTAD

The History of UNCTAD 1964–1984, 1985.

UNCTC

The CTC Reporter. Journal published every six months.

Transnational Corporations in World Development: Trends and Prospects, New York, 1988.

REGIONAL ECONOMIC COMMISSIONS

Economic survey of . . . (region in question) *in 19 . . .* [reporting year].

Addresses

United Nations Conference on Trade and Development
Palais des Nations
1211 Geneva 10
Switzerland

United Nations Centre on Transnational Corporations
United Nations Headquarters
New York, NY 10017
USA

REGIONAL ECONOMIC COMMISSIONS

United Nations Economic Commission for Africa
Adebayo Adedeji
PO Box 3001
Addis Ababa
Ethiopia

United Nations Economic and Social Commission for Asia and the Pacific
United Nations Building
Rajadamnern Avenue
Bangkok 2
Thailand

United Nations Economic Commission for Europe
Palais des Nations
1211 Geneva 10
Switzerland

United Nations Economic Commission for Latin America and the Caribbean
Edificio Naciones Unidas
Avenida Dag Hammarskjöld
Casilla 179-D
Santiago
Chile

United Nations Economic Commission for Western Asia
Mohamed Said Al-Attar
PO Box 27
Baghdad
Iraq

4   The Organisation for Economic Co-operation and Development (OECD)

4.1   Introduction

The Organisation for Economic Co-operation and Development (OECD) which has existed since 1961 is the successor to the Organisation for European Economic Co-operation (OEEC). The latter was set up in 1948, mainly to implement United States Marshall Aid to post-war recovery in Europe. The organisation comprised the non-communist countries of Europe; Canada and the United States were associate members. Apart from the reconstruction of Europe, the liberalisation of international trade and payments was an important aim of the OEEC. With the completion of the reconstruction process and particularly the introduction of convertibility for the European currencies at the end of the 1950s, the OEEC had largely attained its objectives. The subsequent transition to the OECD entailed a number of changes: first, development co-operation was added as a new area. The aim was to co-ordinate aid to developing countries. In addition, Canada and the United States became full members of the organisation. In 1973 membership of the OECD increased to twenty-four with the accession of Japan, Finland, Australia and New Zealand. It was over twenty years later, in 1994, that the membership of the organisation was further increased by the advent of Mexico.

This book is only concerned with those OECD activities which influence international trade.[1] First we shall consider the role of the OEEC/OECD in international trade policy; then we shall examine the position of the OECD in development co-operation, again focusing mainly on the consequences for international trade.

We shall begin with a brief outline of the structure of the OECD as an international organisation. The highest organ is the Council, which generally meets once a year at ministerial level and at other times at ambassador level. Decisions are normally taken according to the principle of unanimity. There is an Executive Committee which prepares the work of the Council and co-ordinates the work of the Committees dealing with specific fields. There is also a Secretariat which does preparatory work,

---

[1] For a general account of the OECD, see A. F. P. Bakker, *International Financial Institutions*, Harlow, 1995 (first published in Amsterdam, 1992), Chapter 8.

conducts studies and produces reports on subjects concerning the OECD. The Secretariat is headed by a Secretary General.

4.2   The OEEC/OECD and international trade policy

The OEEC played an important role in the post-war liberalisation of international trade between member countries. This involved in particular the reduction of quantitative restrictions or quotas: the subject of import tariffs was left to the GATT. In the immediate post-war period, quantitative restrictions were important in balancing imports against the available amount of foreign exchange, which was scarce because of limited scope for exporting, owing to the destruction of production facilities during the war and the large amount of foreign currency needed for reconstruction.

The process of liberalising trade within Europe, in the sense of reducing quotas, began in July 1949, and subsequently received a major boost in 1950 with the introduction of the Code of Liberalisation of Trade. From February 1951, 75 per cent of imports within Europe would have to be quota-free, and no discrimination between member countries was permitted. The establishment of the European Payments Union (EPU) between the OEEC countries in 1950 was also a significant factor in allowing the liberalisation of trade within Europe. The EPU arranged multilateral clearing of the claims and debts resulting from mutual trade.

Thanks to the liberalisation of trade under the OEEC, some 95 per cent of trade within the OEEC was free of quantitative restrictions by 1960, by which time 90 per cent of trade with the dollar area was also liberalised.

Plans for a free-trade area under the OEEC were not successful. On this point there was a split between the six countries which were to form the European Economic Community and the countries which went on to set up the European Free Trade Association (EFTA).

With the establishment of the OECD, there was a change in the international trade policy function. The OECD gradually acquired the role of a consultation forum where trade policy questions could be considered without any actual international agreements having to be concluded as a direct consequence: that remained primarily a matter for the GATT. The OECD is thus a 'gateway' to the GATT/WTO as far as the industrial countries are concerned. Below are some examples of the OECD activities relevant to this context.

In the 1970s the established industrial nations increasingly faced the problem of competition from the developing countries, which were struggling free from the traditional pattern of the international division of labour between developing and developed countries, in which the former produce commodities which they exchange for industrial products from the latter group. The OECD paid a great deal of attention to this process of the rise of the Newly Industrialising Economies, which are rapidly taking on the production and export of industrial products; initially simple, labour-intensive products but later more advanced products, too, for example in the electronics sector (see also Chapter 2). As regards the desired reaction by OECD countries to the new competition, the OECD argued in favour of positive adjustment policies. This meant rejecting a defensive policy aimed at preserving the threatened sectors by protective measures, often the first impulse in this type of case. Positive adjustment means aiding the adjustment process of switching from sectors where the comparative advantage has been lost to new sectors where competition is still possible or where a comparative advantage can be developed. Promotion of the market mechanism plays a leading role here, with the switch from labour as a factor of production being very important in the OECD countries. In order to ease this process, it is important to offer information on job opportunities in other sectors, to provide facilities for retraining, and to encourage mobility of labour in the sense of moving to different regions. National policy in the OECD countries should be geared to this.

Another example of OECD activities in the trade policy sphere concerns the agricultural sector. In the 1970s and 1980s there were repeated conflicts in this sector between the OECD countries themselves and between those nations and the developing countries as a result of the distortion of international trade caused by national support measures in OECD countries. In many cases, those measures led to production surpluses which had to be dumped on the world market with export subsidies, to the detriment of the interests of countries which do not subsidise their exporters. Moreover, this policy exerted downward pressure on world market prices, destroying the incentive to produce agricultural products in developing countries, while those countries – and especially those in Africa – are precisely where production needs to be improved in order to end chronic food shortages.

In 1982 the OECD Council took the initiative in having the agriculture question examined by two committees, the Agriculture Committee and the Trade Committee. At the same time, methods of achieving a balanced, gradual reduction in agricultural protection were also to be analysed. The committees produced their report[2] in 1987, and it was subsequently approved by the Council. An important aspect of the report was that it devised a method of reducing the effects of the various national measures to a common denominator, thus making them comparable and, eventually, negotiable. The criteria developed were the Producer Subsidy Equivalent and the Consumer Subsidy Equivalent, which together measure the effect of national policy measures. The Producer Subsidy Equivalent of a particular policy measure means the payment which would be required to compensate farmers for the loss of income that would occur if the measure were abolished. The Consumer Subsidy Equivalent means the consumption tax or subsidy resulting from a particular policy measure. With the aid of these terms it is also possible to examine the effects of agricultural policy on the production and consumption of agricultural products and hence international trade,[3] and consequently also on world market prices of those products. Thus, it is also possible to analyse the influence on world market prices of a reduction in agricultural support in the OECD countries. The OECD study showed that the effects might be considerable. Thus, a 10 per cent cut in support for the dairy sector could lead to a 6 per cent increase in the world market price.

---

[2] OECD, *National Policies and Agricultural Trade*, Paris, 1987.
[3] Because production minus consumption of a product in a country is, by definition, equal to the country's exports of that product, or imports if the amount is negative.

Box 4.1: Van Lennap on the OECD's 'battle against fossilisation'

In his biography published in 1991, Emile van Lennep, who was Secretary General of the OECD from 1969 to 1984, recounts this organisation's battle against fossilisation as a result of a defensive reaction to changes in the world economy, such as the oil crisis and the rise of the Newly Industrialising Countries. He tells how the term 'positive adjustment policy' is devised as a more polite alternative to the advice 'hands off'. He also mentions a political blunder by the OECD Secretariat, which included Japan among the Newly Industrialising Countries in the first version of a report. Japan was so offended that it initially demanded that the whole report be withdrawn, but Van Lennep managed to get the report published after all, albeit without any reference to Japan.

Source: E. van Lennep and E. Schoorl, *Emile van Lennep in the world economy: memories of an international Dutchman*, Leiden, 1991, pp. 260–2.

These examples of the OECD's activities in the international trade policy sphere clearly reflect how the OECD is constantly developing into an organisation which strives to keep market mechanisms working and to prevent the fossilisation of existing economic structures.[4]

These examples might give the impression that the OECD only performs the function of a research institute and prepares the ground for concrete negotiations within other international organisations. That impression would be incorrect: there are also examples of activities which have produced concrete results within the OECD itself. Here we shall discuss a number of activities which are relevant to international trade. The first concerns the environment problem, and particularly the possible consequences for the competitive positions of individual countries. In 1974, after preparatory work by the Environment Committee, the OECD Council issued a Declaration on the Guiding Principles concerning the International Economic Aspects of Environmental Policies. Here, the OECD countries commit themselves to the Polluter Pays Principle (sometimes abbreviated to PPP), on the basis that, if all OECD countries adhere to this principle, it will be possible to prevent environmental policy from distorting competitive positions. Undesirable distortion of competitive relationships could occur if, for example, some countries were to give companies subsidies to help them to control the environmental damage which they cause, and other countries made the companies themselves pay the bill. In other words, the Polluter Pays Principle means that, in principle, companies are not given any environmental subsidies. The Guiding Principles do, however, stipulate some exceptions to this, such as government support for environmental research.

Another activity concerns multinational corporations. Chapter 3 has already described the background to the involvement of international organisations with such

---

[4] See also A. F. P. Bakker, *International Financial Institutions*, Harlow, 1995 (first published Amsterdam, 1992; see especially. pp. 124–5).

corporations in the discussion of the United Nations' activities in connection with them. While the UN has not yet got any farther than a draft code of conduct for transnational corporations, the OECD Council agreed a Declaration on International Investment and Multinational Enterprises as long ago as 1976, to which were annexed Guidelines for Multinational Enterprises. Although the guidelines are not legally enforceable, they do have influence as recommendations by the joint governments of the OECD countries to multinationals operating in the OECD area. Like the subsequent UN draft code of conduct dating from 1988, the OECD guidelines state the principle that internal transfer prices should correspond to prices prevailing on external markets (the arm's length principle).

At the same time as adopting the Declaration, the OECD Council decided to apply the principle of national treatment to multinationals. This means that if a foreign company from one OECD country is established in another OECD country, it is subject to the same laws and regulations as a domestic company. As already stated in Chapter 3, the OECD rules deviate in this respect from the UN draft code of conduct, which refers to fair and equitable treatment.

Another achievement worth mentioning is the Arrangement on Guidelines for Officially Supported Credits, popularly known as the OECD Consensus, which was set up by the OECD in 1978. It has the status of a gentleman's agreement between the OECD countries, and not that of an OECD Council decision. The Consensus aims to establish limits to competition between OECD countries as regards involvement by the government or government bodies in the provision of export credits on favourable terms. It includes agreements on maximum repayment periods and minimum interest payments, the latter being constantly adapted to financial market trends.

The last example of practical activity connected with international trade is the formation of the International Energy Agency (IEA) in 1974 by the OECD countries – except for France – in response to the first oil crisis unleashed by OPEC at the end of 1973 (see also Chapter 5). Organisationally, the IEA is part of the OECD. It has effectively been created by a bloc of consumer countries to oppose the producers' cartel, OPEC. Under the IEA there were agreements on the allocation of oil stocks of member countries in the case of another crisis concerning the availability of oil. In the longer term, the policy is aimed at reducing demand for energy.

4.3 The OECD and development co-operation

As already stated, development co-operation was the most important new sphere of activity when the OECD was established. The intention was to find ways of increasing and improving the flow of financial resources to developing countries in order to make aid more effective and to co-ordinate national aid programmes. The central role here is played by the Development Assistance Committee (DAC), in which the OECD donor countries participate. An important role is played by 'confrontations' over the policy pursued by the various DAC members, a method which is also used in other spheres by the OECD, including the general economic policy of member countries. An attempt is made to improve policy quality by critical examination of members' policy in mutual discussions.

The development co-operation aspect which is particularly important in this book is that of tied development aid, which means that the recipient country is obliged to spend the development money in the donor country. Thus, tied aid is located at the interface between development policy and trade policy in the sense of export promotion.

Where tied aid means that a higher price has to be paid for supplies than if aid were given without restrictions on where to spend it – and that will often be the case – the real value of the aid is reduced by being tied. For the DAC, reducing the tying of aid is an important issue, but the process is a difficult one. A recent development which may represent a step forward is the 'Helsinki package' dating from 1991, which concerns both tied aid and officially supported export credits. The agreement should be seen as an amendment to the Consensus regarding officially supported export credits, discussed in the preceding section, and also has the same legal status. It was agreed that, with the exception of aid to the least developed countries, projects which are commercially viable if financed on market terms or terms which are permissible under the Consensus are not eligible for financing by tied aid. The idea here is that flows of non-commercial finance in the form of development aid should, as far as possible, lead to *additional* availability of resources in the recipient countries, and should not amount to the replacement of commercial finance by development aid, which would not ultimately produce any increase in the flow of finance. Another positive aspect is the effort to distinguish between export promotion policy and development policy in the donor countries, since different considerations should, in principle, play a role in these areas.

4.4   The future of the OECD

From time to time people wonder what lies ahead for the OECD as an international organisation. During 1994 the question arose again, prompted by the accession of Mexico as the twenty-fifth member and the issue of the successor to the Frenchman Jean-Claude Paye as Secretary General. Some people see signs that the OECD's importance is declining, and refer, for example, to the fact that in 1989 it was the European Commission that was asked to co-ordinate aid to the East European countries, helping them make the transition from a planned economy to a market economy (see also Chapter 7). Since this involved co-ordinating aid given not just by EC members but also by other OECD countries, the OECD would have been a more obvious choice as the co-ordinating body. Another point is that some people regard the quality of the studies produced by OECD staff as inadequate compared with those of organisations such as the IMF and the World Bank. However, an important study was published in 1994 on the unemployment problem in the OECD area and a possible solution to it.[5]

Although opinions differ on the future importance of the OECD, it is clear that this organisation will always tend, by nature, to operate in the background to some extent, so that it cannot brandish spectacular achievements in the way that the GATT can, for example. Thus, the successful conclusion of the Uruguay Round can be said to give the world economy a boost worth several hundred billion dollars once the agreements are implemented. Nevertheless, staying with the specific example of the Uruguay Round, the OECD did play an important role in changing countries' attitudes so that they were willing to tackle the protectionist agricultural policies, a key aspect of the round.

Bibliography

McBean, A. I. and Snowden, P. N. *International Institutions in Trade and Finance*, London, 1981, especially Chapter 7.

Van Meerhaeghe, M. A. G., *International Economic Institutions*, Harlow, 1971, especially Chapter 6.

OECD publications relevant to international trade

Activities of OECD in 19 . . . [reporting year]. Annual report of the Secretary General.

Development Co-operation, Efforts and Policies of the Members of the Development Assistance Committee. Annual report.

OECD Observer. Magazine published every two months with articles on new developments in the OECD and the background to them.

The Case for Positive Adjustment Policies, a Compendium of OECD Documents, 1978/79, 1979.

The Export Credit Financing System in OECD Member Countries, 1990.

The Impact of the Newly Industrialising Countries on Production and Trade in Manufactures. Report by the Secretary General, 1979. (In 1988 a sequel to this report was published under the title *The Newly Industrialising Countries: Challenge and Opportunity for OECD Countries*.)

National Policies and Agricultural Trade, 1987

The OECD Guidelines for Multinational Enterprises, 1986.

Address

Organisation for Economic Co-operation and Development
2 Rue André Pascal
75775 Paris, Cedex 16
France

---

[5] OECD, *The OECD Jobs Study*, Paris, 1994.

5 International institutions concerned with international trade in commodities

5.1 Background

Over the years, special arrangements have applied to trade in commodities on account of the specific characteristics of these products. Chapter 3 has already considered this in the context of the developing countries issue. Two central problems emphasised there were the instability of commodity prices and the long-term trend in the relationship between prices of commodities and prices of industrial products. This chapter will examine these questions and possible solutions in greater depth.

The instability of commodity prices, or more precisely the great variability of prices over time, can be explained in economic theory on the basis of low price elasticities of commodity demand and supply, particularly in the short term. An example may explain what this means. In the case of agricultural products, supply is dependent in the short term, i.e. within one growing season, on decisions taken at the start of the season, and thus cannot be altered quickly. Demand for agricultural products will not change greatly if the price changes: many products of this type are basic necessities whose consumption is not very price-sensitive. If a shock occurs in such a market, e.g. in the form of a reduced supply owing to a failed harvest, it will lead to a sharp rise in prices, which will hardly be inhibited at all by a reduction in demand.

As regards the long-term trend in commodity prices in relation to prices of industrial products, the central point in the discussion, as we have already seen in Chapter 3, is whether or not the terms of trade between commodities and industrial products are tending to deteriorate. As we also saw in Chapter 3, the names of Hans Singer and Raul Prebisch are associated with the thesis of a deteriorating trend. The discussion of this proposition concerns two questions: whether or not the alleged deterioration in the relative price of commodities is in fact taking place (the empirical aspect) and what the reason is for this trend (the theoretical aspect).

As regards the empirical side of the debate, there are several complications that may explain why the proposition that commodity prices are constantly deteriorating relative to the prices of industrial products is so hotly contested. First, frequent use is made of figures which show the trend in *countries'* commodity terms of trade, i.e. the relationship between the country's export and import prices: if the ratio is rising, the terms of trade are said to be improving. The country can then obtain more units of imports per unit of exports. In principle, this concept of the terms of trade is different from that concerning the ratio of commodity prices to prices of industrial products. The two concepts would be largely equivalent only in the case of a country whose exports consisted entirely of a representative range of commodities and whose imports comprised only a representative range of industrial products. In research on this subject, supporters of the theory of a deteriorating ratio of commodity prices to prices of industrial products refer, in particular, to available figures on the long-term trend in the commodity terms of trade of the United Kingdom.[1] The idea behind this is that Britain imports a wide range of commodities and exports a wide range of industrial products, so that the trend in its terms of trade can be seen as a reflection of the trend in commodity prices relative to prices of industrial products, in that an improvement in the British terms of trade would reflect a reduction in the relative price of commodities and vice versa. On the basis of these figures, one can conclude that there was a downward trend in relative commodity prices from the end of the nineteenth century to the eve of World War II.

There are a number of problems with this approach. The most pressing question is: are the British figures representative? Other studies have shown, for example, that the trend in the UK's terms of trade has differed greatly from that of other industrial countries which can equally be considered to import a wide range of commodities and export a wide range of industrial products. Another problem is the failure to take account of the fact that British import prices include transport costs (imports are generally priced on a *cif* basis, i.e. including cost, insurance and freight). These costs have fallen sharply during the period under consideration, so that the decline in the relative price of commodities is over-estimated. Another type of problem concerns the general difficulty of working with price index numbers which show the trend in prices of a basket of goods from a base year. The picture which emerges is often greatly affected by the choice of base year.

In all, it must be said that the empirical correctness of the proposition that commodity prices are tending to decline relative to prices of industrial products is far from proven.

If we next briefly consider how the alleged trend can be explained in theory, then one of the first factors is the lower income-elasticity of demand for commodities compared to industrial products. This means that, as global incomes rise, growth in demand for commodities, and consequently the trend in prices, stays behind. Another reason often put forward is the difference between the form of markets in developed and in developing countries. This concerns the labour market in particular. In the industrial countries, trade unions are powerful enough to translate productivity improvements into wage increases so that, all other things being equal, the prices of the final products remain unchanged, whereas in developing countries trade unions have less power or are totally absent, so that productivity improvements lead to lower product prices.

---

[1] See for example G. M. Meier, *International Trade and Development*, New York, 1963, especially Chapter 3, and D. Sapsford, 'The Debate over Trends in the Terms of Trade', in D. Greenaway (ed.), *Economic Development and International Trade*, Basingstoke and London, 1988, pp. 117–31.

It is useful to be aware of the meaning of an improvement in a country's terms of trade. Although this indicates that the purchasing power of a unit of a country's exports is rising in terms of imports, an excessive increase in the price of a country's exports may be detrimental to sales in terms of export volume. If sales react strongly to the price rise – i.e. if foreign demand for the country's exports is elastic – export earnings may actually fall. This means that an improvement in the terms of trade is not necessarily beneficial for a country, and that a deterioration in the terms of trade may be preferable from the point of view of a country's competitive position. As we saw before, commodities are often characterised by a relatively inelastic demand in the short run, so one might conclude that the problem of a deterioration in competitiveness as a result of higher prices is not a serious one. One should be aware, however, that the elasticity of demand is usually considerably higher in the longer run (see also the next section on OPEC).

Over the years, the problems concerning commodity prices have led to different kinds of official intervention to correct the price developments which would occur on the free market. In this connection, the rest of this chapter will consider the following arrangements:

- agreements solely between countries producing a particular commodity, aimed at influencing the market process;
- agreements between producer and consumer countries aimed at intervention in the market process;
- arrangements which consist of retrospective correction of fluctuations in commodity export earnings.

5.2 Co-operation between producers: the OPEC cartel

In the case of certain commodities, producers can come to believe that their product is so essential to its users that, by organising themselves, they can profit from their strong market position and raise their export earnings. Although this kind of attempt had already been made in the period between the two world wars, the most important example is undoubtedly the Organisation of Petroleum Exporting Countries (OPEC), comprising a number of suppliers of crude oil. Although this organisation was set up in 1960, with Iran, Iraq, Kuwait, Saudi Arabia and Venezuela as the original members, its most important period starts in the 1970s when it orchestrated steep increases in crude oil prices. The number of members has since risen to thirteen.

While the OPEC countries, which are all in the developing country category, were initially still heavily dependent on the 'seven sisters', the large Western oil companies, they are gradually beginning to acquire greater control over their oil resources and hence over oil prices. In the first instance, in 1960, the principal aim was stated to be the stabilisation of international oil prices; in 1968 the aim was said to be to prevent a decline in the price relative to that of industrial products, and in 1971 the process of drastic price rises began, the first dramatic step being the quadrupling of the 'posted prices' in December 1973 in relation to the prices announced in June of that same year. Posted prices are the prices which sellers of a product, in this case the OPEC countries together, set for the sale of their product.

After a few years of relative stability in oil prices, a new round of very sharp price increases began in 1979–80. Although the resulting price rise was relatively less than that of 1973, it still led to a greater increase in absolute terms.

These massive price increases produce shocks in various ways. First, there are the economic effects, such as the impact on the export earnings of the oil-exporting countries and on the oil bill of the importing countries, the inflationary effect and the depressing effect on global spending because purchasing power is 'leaking' to a group of countries with a low absorption capacity. A second shock concerns the realisation by other developing countries that they may be able to organise themselves in the same way as OPEC. This has led to some practical attempts to set up other producer cartels, e.g. in the case of banana and copper exporters, but they have not been very successful. Third, the oil shock has made the developed countries more willing to conclude international agreements on commodities and other matters important to developing countries. Chapter 3 considered the consequences of this in the context of the activities of UN bodies.

In assessing whether OPEC has been successful from the point of view of its members' aim of massively increasing their export earnings, a distinction has to be made between the short term and the longer term. In the short term, the conditions for a successful price cartel were fulfilled. One primary condition is that the cartel members must have a substantial degree of control over the total market supply, and retain that control in spite of the price increase: the price elasticity of supply from non-cartel members must be low. In our case, OPEC represented 53.5 per cent of the world's crude oil production.[2] A second important point is that demand for the product offered by the cartel must be so inelastic that earnings actually rise as a result of the price increase. In the case of oil, this condition was met in the short term, because in the short term it is not possible to take measures to cut oil consumption or switch to other sources of energy. A third condition concerns the cartel's cohesion: there must be a willingness to limit supplies jointly in such a way that the fixed prices can actually be maintained.

In the longer term, however, forces emerged which undermined the power of OPEC. As regards the first factor mentioned above, OPEC's share of world production, a substantial change took place over the years. The higher price of oil made sources in other countries viable and stimulated the exploration process: examples of new suppliers were the United Kingdom and Norway, with their (relatively expensive) North Sea oil. The share of the OPEC countries in world oil production fell from 53.5 per cent in 1973 to 30 per cent in 1985.

On the demand side there is also a difference between the short term and the long term. In the longer term, research into energy-saving techniques bears fruit. A switch

---

[2] The figures in this section are taken from various issues of the IMF's *World Economic Outlook*.

Figure 5.1 Crude oil prices, 1970–93 (dollars per barrel)

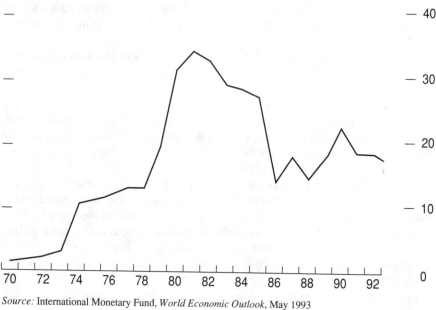

Source: International Monetary Fund, *World Economic Outlook*, May 1993

to other sources of energy such as natural gas is also only possible in the longer term because time-consuming investments are often necessary, such as laying pipelines. Between 1973 and 1985, this type of development led to a 20 per cent decline in consumption of crude oil by industrial countries, by far the most important group of consumers. Problems also arose within OPEC with regard to cohesion, the most dramatic instances being the war between Iraq and Iran in the 1980s and the conflict following Iraq's occupation of Kuwait. These and other mutual conflicts seriously hindered the agreements on restricting production which were necessary to maintain the high price level.

In all, the power of the OPEC cartel was gradually eroded, leading to less control over oil prices. This is clear from Figure 5.1, which shows how the sharp increase in the oil price was largely eliminated during the 1980s.

5.3 Agreements between producer and consumer countries on intervention in commodity markets

The previous section concerned commodity producers trying to raise the price of their commodity: this one will examine International Commodity Agreements (ICAs) which involve producer and consumer countries. Agreements are reached on the stabilisation of the price of a particular commodity, the idea being that this stabilises export earnings for producer countries while consumer countries can be more certain of the price to be paid.

Price stabilisation agreements generally involve agreeing a minimum and a maximum price which limit market price movements. There are various ways of preventing market prices from actually going beyond the set margins. One possibility is for the agreement to contain a guarantee that the producer country will offer agreed quantities of the commodity in question once the maximum price is reached, and the consumer countries will purchase agreed quantities once the minimum price is reached. This arrangement is known as a multilateral contract and was applied in the first version of the International Wheat Agreement dating from 1949. Another possibility is to stabilise the price via a buffer stock. If the price reaches the maximum level, then the agency controlling the buffer stock places some of it on the market to increase the supply, while the buffer stock authority increases its demand when the minimum price is reached. One example of use of the buffer stock system was the International Tin Agreement. In such a system, the margin between the maximum and minimum price should ideally be such that the buffer stock is sufficiently large to counteract strong price rises, but does not become too large (and hence too expensive) if the market price has to be supported. This must mean that the price margin is around the market equilibrium price in the long term. This also applies to the multilateral contract discussed before.

Another way of stabilising commodity prices is via an export quota system: each producer country belonging to the system is allocated a certain maximum quantity of exports. This should maintain the price level: if the commodity price nevertheless falls, the quota can be adjusted downwards. This system was applied in agreements on international trade in coffee and sugar. One objection to the export quota system is that only the exports of participating producer countries are limited, and not their output. When output is high, this may lead to part of it being left 'hanging over the market', encouraging the expectation that, sooner or later, the surplus production will have to be released anyway. This may make a price cut seem imminent, causing speculators to act in such a way as to help bring it about. A second problem of the export quota system is that it is very difficult to alter quotas once they have been set, if circumstances change – for example, if new suppliers should arise. The established suppliers have an interest in maintaining the old allocation, and this can lead to rigidity in such a system.

Export quotas are also applied in combination with a buffer stock, particularly in situations where stocks are growing excessively. The tin sector was one example of this.

With the present type of commodity agreements, it is not possible to maintain a price which is too high or too low relative to its long-term equilibrium. The effects are most evident in the buffer stock system: if the minimum price is set too high, the buffer stock will become too large, leading to high financing costs, while if the maximum price is too low the buffer stock will soon be exhausted. Another complication is that, if prices are out of balance, speculators will often guess the fact and, by their actions, quickly reveal that the prices cannot be maintained.

This brings us to the most fundamental problem of international commodity agreements, namely that it is very difficult if not impossible to *predict* the equilibrium price of a commodity in the long term. Naturally, the price margin can be adjusted from time to time, but if this is done too often the agreement will fail in its objective.

Another essential problem of commodity agreements is that commodity producers are inclined to use them to achieve higher prices, i.e. prices above the long-term market equilibrium price. Thus, the agreement is doomed from the start because it cannot function with the wrong price range.

There are also a number of other problems relating to international commodity agreements. Thus, it cannot simply be assumed that the stabilisation of a commodity's price also means stabilisation of the exporting countries' export earnings. An important factor here is whether the potential change in the commodity price is due to changes on the demand side or the supply side. In the latter case, in the absence of price stabilisation, there is (partial) automatic stabilisation of earnings: this does not occur in the former case. For example, if the supply declines, the resulting fall in earnings will be offset by a rise in the price of the commodity, at least if the supplier concerned is a substantial market participant. In contrast, if demand falls, the resulting drop in earnings will be aggravated by a decline in the price of the commodity. Thus, price stabilisation will only lead to stabilisation of export earnings for commodities whose prices change largely as a result of changes in demand, e.g. commodities for which demand is sensitive to cyclical trends. For commodities such as many agricultural products which are subject to fluctuations in supply, price stabilisation would not have the desired result of stabilising export earnings, and could even have a destabilising effect.

A problem with commodity agreements which makes them difficult to conclude is that the interests of producer countries are opposed to those of consumer countries. In a period of high commodity prices, consumer countries will have an interest in an agreement but producers will not, whereas if prices are low, the roles are reversed. It is then necessary for both parties to be aware of the longer-term advantages, regardless of the actual price situation at the time.

An additional complication of commodity agreements, which has arisen since the end of the global system of fixed exchange rates in 1973, is that the stabilisation of the price of a commodity will often mean that the dollar price is kept within certain limits, as the dollar is the currency in which prices are quoted on most commodity markets. Owing to exchange-rate fluctuations between the dollar and other currencies, stabilisation of the dollar price does not automatically also mean stabilisation of the price in another currency, which may be more relevant to a commodity exporter.

The problems discussed above concerning international commodity agreements are part of the reason why, although plans for a whole series of commodity agreements with joint finance were made during the 1970s in the debate on the New International Economic Order (see Chapter 3), those plans were never actually implemented and existing agreements such as that on tin (see Box 5.1) broke down.

> # Box 5.1: The vicissitudes of the international tin agreements
>
> International agreements on the tin market have a long history going back to before World War II. The first attempts by a number of producers to control the tin market date from 1921. This Bandoeng Pool wanted to stabilise the price via a buffer stock, in this case called a pool. In 1931 an International Tin Agreement was concluded which combined a buffer stock with quotas to limit supplies.
>
> After an interruption due to World War II, a new International Tin Agreement was concluded in 1954 which now also involved consumer countries. This again comprised a buffer stock, if necessary in combination with export restrictions to support the price. The agreement was renewed several times.
>
> For a long time it was thought that the successive tin agreements were reasonably effective in stabilising the price of tin, although the stabilising role of the US in buying and selling strategic stockpiles was important from time to time. Nevertheless, in 1985 the tin agreement was ended, after years of net purchases to support the floor price. Excessive risks were incurred by operating partly on borrowed money and by risky transactions on the futures market. However, the essential problem was that the floor price was set too high. Thus, the collapse of the tin agreement illustrates the basic problem of commodity agreements, which is to do with setting an equilibrium floor and ceiling price.

5.4 Compensation schemes for export earnings shortfall

Another way of helping to stabilise export earnings from commodities is to supplement them retrospectively by some kind of compensatory financing system. The great advantage of this is that there is no need to interfere with the price mechanism, in the manner of the international commodity agreements mentioned above; the associated problems are thus avoided. On the other hand, compensatory financing does have its problems, too. The principal one is that the exporting countries may be tempted into deliberately limiting their supply in order to collect compensation, which is not of course intended for such cases. Safeguards need to be incorporated in the form of specific rules to prevent this.

Over the years, many compensatory financing schemes have been proposed. Only two schemes actually in operation will be discussed here. The first is the Compensatory Financing Facility (CFF), which was added to the financial facilities of the International Monetary Fund in 1963. Through this facility, a country whose export earnings fall below the medium-term trend in a particular year, for reasons beyond the control of the country itself, can obtain a loan from the Fund.[3] The idea is

---

[3] For an explanation of all the IMF credit facilities, see A. F. P. Bakker, *International Financial Institutions*, Harlow, 1995 (first published Amsterdam, 1992), Chapter 2.

that the loans can subsequently be redeemed in years when export earnings exceed the trend. Thus, with the aid of this facility it is possible to overcome periods of difficulty. The facility was created for developing countries which are heavily dependent on commodity exports, though it is formally open to all IMF members.

The maximum 'drawing' on the IMF under the CFF has been increased over the years: initially it was only 25 per cent of the quota of the country concerned, but since 1988 the maximum which may be drawn is 122 per cent of the quota. This limit relates to the enlarged facility, the Compensatory and Contingency Financing Facility (CCFF) which can also be used to obtain credit in the case of other external shocks, such as an increase in the prices of certain essential imports and a rise in interest rates, or a drop in earnings from tourism. Once again, these are events which are not caused by the country itself.

In implementing the scheme, the IMF checks whether the decline in export earnings is not actually attributable to the country itself. If a drop in the market price is the main reason for the decline, the case is often clear-cut. If the reason is a decline in the volume of exports, closer investigation is needed. If the drop in volume proves to have been brought about by the country itself, by retention of stocks in anticipation of higher prices, for example, then the permitted use of the facility is adjusted to allow for that.

The other compensatory financing scheme to be discussed here is the STABEX system introduced in 1975 under the Lomé Convention between the European Community and former colonies of EC countries in Africa, the Caribbean and the Pacific, known as the ACP states. The STABEX system differs from the IMF scheme in a number of respects. As we have already seen, the scheme applies only to a limited group of countries, and then only to their exports to the EC. STABEX also concerns export earnings of *individual* commodities which fall below the trend: the system originally listed thirteen such products. Thus, a country can, in principle, obtain compensation for the decline in earnings from one particular commodity while earnings from other commodities are increasing. This is known as the gross method, while the IMF facility applies a net method which considers export earnings across the board. Another difference is that the STABEX payments are grants, in the case of ACP states deemed to be in the category of least developed countries, and interest free loans for the rest of the group, whereas the IMF payments are loans on which interest is payable. One last difference to be discussed here is that STABEX payments are subject to a limit for each five-year period, which may mean that resources have been exhausted at any particular moment, whereas the IMF financing facility only imposes limits on the level to which individual countries may use the scheme, but no limit on the overall use of the facility by all eligible countries.

The differences between the two schemes may explain why, in practice, ACP states sometimes obtain funds from the IMF's CCFF instead of the STABEX scheme. In other cases the reverse happens, with payments being made to ACP states under STABEX but not under the Fund facility.

In 1979, under the Second Lomé Convention, a scheme similar to STABEX was introduced for mineral products, under the name of SYSMIN. On this occasion, and also when the Lomé Convention was subsequently renewed or revised, the number of commodities covered by the STABEX scheme was extended. Another change, implemented in 1989 when Lomé IV was concluded is that funds in future will be provided in the form of grants only. The resources will not be made available until the EC and national authorities of the ACP state have agreed on their use.

Bibliography

Goreux, L. M., *Compensatory Financing Facility*, Pamphlet Series No. 34, IMF, Washington DC, 1980.

Greenaway, D. (ed.), *Economic Development and International Trade*, Basingstoke and London, 1988.

Hallwood, P. and Sinclair, S. W., *Oil, Debt and Development: OPEC in the Third World*, London, 1981.

International Monetary Fund, *World Economic Outlook*, in which summaries of oil market trends are published each year (in the spring issue).

Johnson, H. G., *Economic Policies towards Less Developed Countries*, London, 1967.

Meier, G. M., *International Trade and Development*, New York, 1963.

McBean, A. I. and Nguyen, D. T., *Commodity Policies: Problems and Prospects*, Beckenham, 1987.

6   Regional economic integration

6.1   Introduction

After World War II economic integration, in the sense of the elimination of barriers to international competition, took place not only at world level, under the GATT, but also on a regional scale, with Europe taking the lead. This process has intensified in recent times, so much so that some people fear the creation of blocs leading to greater protectionist tendencies. In principle, regional integration can be either a step towards global free trade or a move towards more protectionism in the world.

Before discussing regional integration groupings in various parts of the world, this chapter will look at the various forms of regional economic integration, their effects and the GATT/WTO rules on the subject. Here we are concerned only with the integration of markets of final products and factors of production, or integration in the real sphere; monetary integration is not considered.[1]

Regional economic integration may take various forms: those described here represent successively increasing degrees of economic integration. The forms mentioned relate to economic integration across the board; forms of economic integration for individual sectors, 'sectoral integration', are also possible.

Free trade area. This entails the elimination of tariffs and other measures which restrict trade between participating countries, without any common trade policy being pursued in relation to third countries. The lack of a common external trade policy necessitates measures to prevent imports from outside the area from being channelled via the country with the lowest barriers to imports, because that would undermine the trade policy of countries with a less liberal régime. This is known as *deflection of trade*, and can be prevented by demanding certificates of origin, indicating the country of origin for goods crossing the borders.

Customs union. This form of integration has the additional feature of a common trade policy vis-à-vis third countries, particularly in the form of a common external tariff, i.e. the tariffs on imports from outside the union.

---

[1] See A. F. P. Bakker, *International Financial Institutions*, Harlow, 1995 (first published Amsterdam, 1992; pp. 140–55).

Common market. This form includes movement of the factors of production. In principle, restrictions on such movements between member countries are abolished.

Integrated market or *internal market.* Although a common market in principle allows the free movement of goods (and services) and factors of production – labour and capital – in practice this does not mean that cross-border economic transactions between member countries can proceed totally unhindered. Thus, there may still be differences in national policy, for example, as regards product standards and taxation, which prevent total freedom of movement. Trade is influenced not only by measures explicitly directed at trade, but also by other measures which may produce side-effects in the trade sphere.[2] An integrated market aims to eliminate the remaining barriers as well. Since this form of integration is really only relevant in the context of the economic integration of the European Community/Union, it will be examined in more detail in the section on the EC/EU.

Economic union. This concept is an extension of the integrated market and is often used in combination with monetary union in the combined term Economic and Monetary Union (EMU). Economic union, which is the counterpart to monetary union in the real sphere, is much the same as an integrated market. The additional feature of economic union is that economic policy, including fiscal policy, is co-ordinated sufficiently to permit monetary union.

As regards the effects of regional economic integration, a distinction must first be made between the *static effects*, deemed to occur once only when the integration comes into force, and the *dynamic effects,* which represent a permanent effect on the growth potential of the integrating area.

There are two possible static effects, namely trade creation and trade diversion. The former concerns the creation of new trade as a result of regional economic integration, as foreign suppliers within the area can offer products at lower prices than domestic suppliers. This has positive welfare effects for the member countries without being detrimental to the welfare of the rest of the world.

In the case of trade diversion, imports which used to come from countries not included in the integration arrangement are replaced by imports from a partner country, because the latter benefits from the elimination of tariffs and other trade impediments which remain in force for third countries. In this case there are negative welfare effects for non-member countries; it is not possible to generalise about the welfare effects for countries taking part in integration because they will depend on the circumstances, e.g. as regards the terms-of-trade effects of the integration arrangement.

The terms 'trade creation' and 'trade diversion' can also be used to indicate whether regional integration can be regarded as a step towards global free trade or a move towards more protection in the world. Integration arrangements dominated by trade creation lead to more free trade overall, in contrast to arrangements in which trade diversion is predominant.

---

[2] In this connection, see also the discussion of non-tariff barriers to trade in Chapter 2.

The dynamic effects of regional integration include effects such as economies of scale – i.e. the possibility of producing on a larger scale at lower average cost, permitted by the larger market in the region – and the favourable effects of increased competition within the region.

The GATT/WTO rules on regional free trade are contained in Article XXIV of the GATT; this concerns free-trade areas and customs unions, particularly the conditions under which these can be tolerated as exceptions to the principle of non-discrimination. These conditions are intended to encourage such forms of integration to contribute to worldwide free-trade. Thus, overall, the formation of a free-trade area or customs union must not lead to higher tariffs or other barriers vis-à-vis third countries. Also, co-operation on trade policy should concern 'substantially all trade' of member countries.

As a result of the Tokyo Round of GATT negotiations, Article XXIV has largely ceased to apply to regional economic integration between developing countries, in that those countries have been given greater freedom to determine the form of their mutual integration.

Within the scope of this chapter it is not possible to discuss all the regional economic integration arrangements in the world. First we shall examine instances of integration in developed countries, beginning with the most important, the European Community, or the European Union as it is now called. Next we shall discuss regional economic integration in the rest of Western Europe in the account of the European Free Trade Association and the European Economic Area, followed by regional integration in North America. One regional integration arrangement that will not be considered here is the free trade area between Australia and New Zealand, the ANZCERTA (Australia–New Zealand Closer Economic Relations Trade Agreement). However, a number of regional economic integration arrangements by developing countries will be examined at the end of the chapter.

A co-operative arrangement that will also be omitted is the APEC (Asian–Pacific Economic Co-operation) of countries around the Pacific Basin. Although a number of major countries such as the United States and Japan are involved, this form of co-operation has not (yet) reached the stage where it can be called integration in the sense applied here, which requires at least the conclusion of concrete agreements on trade liberalisation between the countries concerned.

6.2   The European Community/Union[3]

In the period following World War II, consultations on regional free trade in Europe initially took place in the OEEC (see Chapter 4), but in 1951 the European Coal and Steel Community (ECSC) was established by the Treaty of Paris, as the first concrete step for a group of only six countries (Belgium, France, Luxembourg, Netherlands,

---

[3] For a more extensive, general account of the European Community/Union, see A. F. P. Bakker, *International Financial Institutions*, Harlow, 1995 (first published Amsterdam, 1992, pp. 133–40).

Figure 6.1 Article from *The Economist*, 20 November 1993 [ref. p. 128]

EU fugaces labuntur communitates

FROM OUR BRUSSELS CORRESPONDENT

JUST as most people had stopped talking about the "common market" and become used to calling it the European Community, the Maastricht treaty comes along and confuses everyone by creating something called the European Union. What is it, and why has *The Economist* reluctantly decided to abandon the now familiar EC for the something-between-a-sigh-and-an-expletive EU?

The viscosity of the answer reflects that of the Maastricht treaty, which came into force on November 1st, bringing the Union with it. It is yet another masterpiece of Euro-fudge. The new Union is the old Community with two additions. One is a common foreign and security policy; the other is co-operation between the 12 governments in justice and police matters. The rest of what Maastricht is supposed to do—open the road to economic union and a single currency, strengthen the European Parliament, give Brussels new powers over industrial policy, consumer affairs, health and education—stays four-square within the EC.

The whole construction—EC plus foreign and security policy plus justice and police co-operation—adds up to the European Union.

On the other hand, it does not add up to one single decision-taking process but to three separate ones. Moreover, the European Union has no legal persona. Only EC, and/or the member-states, can conclude international agreements, for instance.

In other words, confusion reigns. It certainly does among the Union's architects. At a press conference after the recent Brussels summit, John Major fluffed his first attempt to explain what European Union is and why he would be using the name sparingly. He eventually spoke of a "three-pillared union" within which EC work would continue as before, while anything to do with foreign and security matters or justice and police would be strictly Union business. The main reason for this separation is the desire of several countries, led by Britain and France, to keep the Maastricht additions as much as possible out of the hands of the Brussels commission and the European Parliament. British officials in Brussels say they will try to maintain the distinction in day-to-day European affairs. *The Economist* reckons that effort will be forlorn.

Continued

Some people will go on talking about the community regardless of legal accuracy, others will increasingly refer to the Union in all contexts except historical ones. We have decided to opt for the Union, believing (perhaps wrongly) that in time this term will prevail.

We have not had much help from the authorities in reaching our decision. On November 8th the Council of Ministers, the Community's main decision-taking body, became the "Council of Ministers of the European Union". But on November 17th the commission in Brussels evaded the question by rebaptising itself the "European Commission", which nearly everybody thought was its name anyway. The judges of the European court in Luxembourg, conservatives to a man, have decided to remain the "Court of Justice of the European Communities", a reminder that the European Coal and Steel Community and the Atomic Energy Community still exist.

Newspapers are split. Some, like *Le Monde* of Paris and the *Financial Times* of London, have decided simply to replace EC with EU. Germany's *Handelsblatt* seems to have a fair sprinkling of both EUs and ECs. Italy's *La Repubblica* has stuck firmly with the Community. Reuters, in common with the Associated Press and Agence France-Presse, says it will go on using EC for the time being so as not to confuse needlessly its worldwide subscribers. Two of the main American-run newspapers in Europe, the *International Herald Tribune* and the *Wall Street Journal Europe*, have also decided to soldier on with the EC.

Italy and West Germany). This was a form of sectoral economic integration aimed at establishing free trade in the coal and steel sector only. An interesting aspect of the ECSC in comparison with the later European Economic Community (EEC) was the stronger supranational structure, with the High Authority having considerable decision-making powers.

In 1957, sectoral integration progressed via the establishment of the European Atomic Energy Community (EURATOM) and a start was made on total economic integration within the European Economic Community (EEC). The executive organ of the EEC and EURATOM became the European Commission, whose powers were more limited, as we have already said, than those of the ECSC High Authority. The Council of Ministers is generally the decision-making body for the EEC and EURATOM in the last instance. The Commission prepares the decisions of the Council and acts as the 'guardian' of the Treaties of Rome whereby the EEC and EURATOM were founded.

In 1967 the ECSC, EEC and EURATOM were combined to form the European Communit*ies*. Since this plural form never really became accepted, the term European Community (EC) will be used here, at least up until 1 November 1993. On that date the name of the integration arrangement was changed to European Union (EU), as a result of the Treaty of Maastricht which has now been ratified by all Member States.

The number of EC/EU members was increased from six to fifteen in four stages: in 1973 the United Kingdom, Ireland and Denmark joined, followed by Greece in 1981 and Spain and Portugal in 1986. In 1994 negotiations on the accession of Finland, Norway, Austria and Sweden to the EU were concluded, but not all four actually became members on 1 January 1995, since in Norway a referendum decided against EU membership.

Table 6.1 Intra-regional exports as % of total exports; EC and EFTA, 1960–90.

Integration grouping	1960	1970	1975	1980	1985	1990
EC (6 members)	34.5	48.9				
EC (10 members)		51.1	50.1	53.5	52.1	
EC (12 members)					54.5	60.4
EFTA	21.1	28.0	35.2	32.6	31.2	28.2

Source: IMF Occasional Paper no. 93, 1992

The aspects of the European Community relevant to this book are the process of economic integration in international trade and the movement of the factors of production, plus Community policy on certain economic sectors, agriculture being the most important here.

The 1957 EEC Treaty stated its objective as the establishment of a common market. There was to be freedom of movement for goods, services, labour and capital within the EEC – the 'four freedoms' – and there was to be a common trade policy with non-members. A customs union was to be established as the first step in this process, whereby trade in goods within the EEC would be freed from import duties and other impediments such as quantitative import restrictions, in combination with a common external trade policy in the form of a common external tariff for imports from non-member states. Completion of the customs union was expected to take twelve years, from 1 January 1958; however, the union became a fact in July 1968, eighteen months before the end of that period.

A great deal of empirical research has been done on the effects of the creation of the EEC customs union. Although the various studies differ in the methods used and the results obtained, there is general agreement that the customs union led to substantial shifts in the pattern of trade for the member countries (see Table 6 1), and that trade creation exceeded trade diversion overall. Trade creation was greatest in the industrial sector, whereas there was substantial trade diversion in the agricultural sector. A striking result of the empirical research is the minimal effect of the customs union on welfare, in quantitative terms, often representing only a few tenths of one per cent of the Community's Gross Domestic Product. However, these are only the static integration effects: research on the quantitative significance of dynamic effects often yields much higher values.

An important aspect of the EC integration process in the international trade sphere concerns the nature of the specialisation between member states resulting from integration. Specialisation has largely taken the form of specialisation *within* industrial sectors, so that much of the trade within the EC consists of intra-industry trade. This trade is very different from *inter*-industry trade, which can be explained by the traditional theory of international trade based on comparative advantage. According to that approach, specialisation takes place with countries concentrating on particular products: the classic Ricardian example here is wine and cloth, in which Portugal and Britain respectively specialise. In contrast, intra-industry trade consists of international trade in which the countries concerned exchange different varieties of products from the same industrial sectors, which they can produce at competitive prices on the basis of economies of scale. Thus, cars are made by various EC countries and traded with other member states. It is often assumed that trade liberalisation accompanied by intra-industry specialisation will operate more smoothly than liberalisation leading to inter-industry specialisation. With intra-industry specialisation, there is no need for whole industries to disappear or shrink as a result of trade liberalisation; only certain activities within sectors will have to cease, while others can expand. These adjustments within sectors can be assumed to be less painful than adjustments between sectors.

The elimination of tariffs and quantitative restrictions on trade within the EC and the creation of the common external tariff still do not mean that trade in goods is totally free within the Community. As far as internal trade is concerned, there are still various types of barrier which hinder cross-border trade. The wish to eliminate these is the reason behind the idea of establishing an integrated or internal market, which developed during the 1980s. The European business world, organised in the Round Table of European Industrialists, was a significant supporter of the elimination of the remaining trade barriers and other non-tariff measures which cause disruption. The European Commission's White Paper dated 1985, *Completion of the Internal Market*, distinguishes three types of barrier: physical, technical and fiscal. Physical barriers consist of customs procedures at the borders, the resulting hold-ups being particularly costly. Technical barriers consist of differences in national norms and standards relating to products. Fiscal barriers result mainly from differences in indirect taxes and excise duties. Other non-tariff barriers which need to be eliminated are differences in national subsidies, discriminatory practices in government procurement and also restrictive business practices in the private sector. The European competition policy needs to be tightened up both to eliminate these restrictive practices and to prevent an excessive concentration of economic power in the internal market.

Progress towards the internal market, commonly known as 'Project 1992' after the target completion date of 31 December 1992, has its legal basis in the Single European Act which came into force in 1987 and is to be regarded as supplementing the EEC Treaty. An important change introduced by the Act is that many decisions which the Council of Ministers needs to take in the process of establishing the internal market can be passed by a qualified majority, whereas unanimity often used to be required in practice. Another important change concerns the process of harmonising norms and standards. Here it used to be assumed that European standards should be developed in every possible sphere; with the advent of the European Act, the philosophy changed to one of mutual recognition of national rules, with only *minimum* requirements being defined at European level.

Another aspect of the creation of the EC's integrated market concerns external trade policy. Although, as already stated, the EC became a customs union as long ago as 1968, external trade policy really only comprised a common external tariff. As far as non-tariff measures are concerned, the different member states still often have national measures; this is true of the motor vehicle import rules, for example. With the establishment of a 'Europe without borders' at the end of 1992, it was necessary for the EC to tackle external trade measures, because otherwise the EC countries with the most liberal import policies could act as 'funnels' for imports from third countries. Via the relatively open EC countries the goods in question could then enter the internal market. As regards the establishment of an EC policy on imports, the EC's trading partners more than once expressed the fear that a 'Fortress Europe' could be created if European trade policy were to be geared more closely to that of the most protectionist EC countries rather than that of the more liberal member states.

At present it is difficult to ascertain whether a Fortress Europe is actually being erected. For example, in the motor vehicle sector mentioned earlier, national VERs on Japanese exports to the EC were converted to an EC-wide monitoring arrangement whereby, on the one hand, the volume restriction on Japanese car exports to the EC is maintained but, on the other hand, the restriction will be ended by the year 2000.

Having so far concentrated mainly on developments in the EC relating to trade in goods, we shall now examine developments in trade in services and the movement of labour and capital. As already stated, the establishment of a common market, i.e. including free trade in services and free movement of the factors of production, was already the stated objective of the EEC Treaty of 1957. Although significant steps towards liberalisation were taken as a result of that treaty in the sphere of services and factors of production, many impediments still remained. In this connection, a special characteristic of international trade in services is that it is often only possible via a physical presence in the customer country, as we saw in Chapter 2. As in the case of financial services, for example, that presence may be dependent on national licences which are not available to foreign financial institutions. As regards international movement of the factors of production, examples of remaining obstacles are that labour is subject to restrictions owing to non-recognition of qualifications gained in other member states, and financial capital is subject to continuing restrictions on international capital movements in certain countries, such as France and Italy. The aim of 'Project 1992' is to achieve freedom of movement for services and factors of production, or in other words, to complete the development of the EC as a common market by supplementing the measures aimed at establishing free internal trade in goods.

The expected welfare effects of the completion of the internal market in the EC have been assessed on behalf of the European Commission; a summary was published in the *Cecchini Report* and a full account in the *Emerson Report*.[4] It was predicted that the EC's real Gross Domestic Product would be permanently increased by between 4.8 and 6.4 per cent. The most important components of the overall effect are the 'market integration' effects, i.e. the effects resulting from economies of scale and increased competition. These effects are similar to those discussed previously under the heading of 'dynamic effects' in connection with the welfare effects of the creation of the customs union.

---

[4] P. Cecchini, *The European Challenge*, 1992, Aldershot, 1988; M. Emerson *et al.*, *The Economics of 1992: the EC Commission's Assessment of the Economic Effects of Completing the Internal Market*, Oxford, 1988.

To conclude this section, there are two aspects of the EC/EU's economic integration which need to be considered, namely the Common Agricultural Policy and the special trade agreements with countries or groups of countries.

The Common Agricultural Policy is based on the 1957 EEC Treaty and, under that Treaty, its objective is to ensure a fair standard of living for the agricultural community, to stabilise markets, to increase agricultural productivity and to assure the availability of agricultural products while maintaining reasonable prices for the consumer. For this purpose, a market regulation system was set up which offered guaranteed prices for a number of agricultural products; if necessary, prices are maintained by buying up agricultural products (intervention). Prices are uniform throughout the Community. Since they are higher than world market prices, the internal market has to be protected against external competition. This is done by a system of variable levies which offset the difference between world prices and internal prices. As a result, foreign suppliers cannot offer their products on the EC market at prices below the fixed internal EC price and thus compete with suppliers from within the EC. Export subsidies are applied so that goods can be exported to the world market in spite of the high prices.

In some respects the European Agricultural Policy is highly successful, particularly as regards meeting Europe's own demand for agricultural products; the high guaranteed prices are a strong incentive for agricultural production. On the other hand, the system has become increasingly expensive for both consumers and the EC, precisely because of its success in stimulating supplies: a very high proportion of the EC budget is spent on the agricultural sector. The increased production results in surpluses which have to be financed out of EC funds. Exports to the world market are only possible with higher and higher export subsidies, because the increased EC production depresses world market prices, thus increasing the difference in relation to the EC price that has to be bridged by export subsidies. Moreover, this leads to trade policy tension with world market competitors who do not themselves subsidise their agricultural sector, or only to a lesser extent. Over the years, on account of these developments, there were plans to revise the Common Agricultural Policy, the most drastic step so far having been the package of reforms put forward by the then agricultural commissioner, Ray MacSharry from Ireland, which was accepted by the European agriculture ministers in May 1992. One feature of this package was a change in policy, favouring income support for the agricultural sector rather than the price support hitherto applied. Retrospective income support does not affect the pricing process, so that the disruptive effects of artificial prices can be avoided. The distinction here is similar to that which we saw in Chapter 5 when discussing the various methods of stabilising commodity export earnings: commodity agreements which interfere with the market process, or compensatory financing which avoids such interference.

The ongoing reform of EC agricultural policy has now had a beneficial effect on relations with other agricultural exporters; witness the bilateral agreement on the liberalisation of trade in agricultural products concluded with the United States in November 1992 in connection with the GATT Uruguay Round (the Blair House Accord), which was subsequently included in the final agreement on the Uruguay Round at the end of 1993.

Finally, we should consider the special trade policy rules applied by the EU to various countries or groups of countries. These rules apply in addition to those in force under the GATT/WTO and the Generalised System of Preferences for developing countries.

ACP countries. Under consecutive Lomé Agreements, a system of non-reciprocal tariff preferences for imports into the EC applies to these former colonies of EC countries in Africa, the Caribbean and the Pacific. In addition, there is a special scheme for products covered by the European Common Agricultural Policy. In this connection, there is also the STABEX scheme to stabilise earnings from commodity exports. This scheme was discussed in Chapter 5.

Mediterranean countries. The EC has established various types of trade policy arrangement with countries bordering the Mediterranean. Co-operation agreements have been concluded with Morocco, Algeria, Tunisia, Egypt, Lebanon, Jordan, Syria and Yugoslavia which, as regards trade policy, comprise non-reciprocal tariff preferences. There are association agreements with Turkey, Cyprus and Malta which may lead to full EC membership for those countries. The trade advantages under these agreements are therefore, in principle, reciprocal. Progress towards EC membership has been delayed by problems concerning the practical implementation of reciprocity (Cyprus and Malta) and political obstacles (Turkey). Finally, there is a free trade agreement with Israel which is based on full reciprocity.

Central and East European countries. After the political and economic turmoil in Central and Eastern Europe in 1989, consultation began on the liberalisation of trade policy. In the case of Hungary, Poland and what was then still Czechoslovakia, followed later by Bulgaria and Romania, this led to the conclusion of association agreements in the form of 'Europe Agreements'. These may eventually lead to EU membership and, in the trade policy sphere, they are for the time being aimed at reciprocal opening up of markets, although the EC has formulated exceptions for imports of 'sensitive' goods such as agricultural products, textiles/clothing and steel.

There are also special trade arrangements with the EFTA countries, which will be discussed in the next section.

6.3   The European Free Trade Association and the European Economic Area

After the establishment of the EEC, the OEEC continued to discuss the establishment of a free trade area embracing the whole of Western Europe. After the then French President De Gaulle had vetoed that in the autumn of 1958, there were consultations among a number of countries which were thus in danger of being left out. In 1960 this resulted in the adoption of the Stockholm Convention which led to the establishment of the European Free Trade Association (EFTA). The countries taking part were Denmark, Norway, Austria, Portugal, the United Kingdom, Switzerland and Sweden.

As a free trade area, EFTA had a much more lightweight institutional structure than the EC. There was no common trade policy in relation to non-members, nor any common policy on particular sectors, on the lines of the EC agricultural policy, for instance. In fact, trade in agricultural products was also excluded from the EFTA agreements. Thus, EFTA has no supranational bodies: the supreme authority is the Council on which representatives of the member countries have a seat. There are committees to advise the Council on technical matters. Finally, there is a small permanent secretariat. EFTA has its headquarters in Geneva.

EFTA aimed to eliminate tariffs on mutual trade in industrial products within ten years. However, this process was successfully completed more quickly, in six and a half years.

As regards the effects of trade co-operation, an increase in intra-regional trade as a proportion of total trade can also be observed for EFTA (see Table 6.1), especially in the initial period. However, if we consider what influence the trade agreements actually had here in terms of trade creation and trade diversion, and especially the balance of the two, the measured effects are rather small. This is undoubtedly due to the fact that the area of the EFTA countries is not geographically contiguous: changes in the membership of EFTA also played a role here, and there were quite a few of them over the years. In 1961 Finland became an associate member; in 1970, Iceland joined. In 1973 EFTA was dealt a heavy blow when Denmark and the United Kingdom went over to the EC; in 1986 Portugal did the same. Liechtenstein joined the organisation in 1991.

From this it is already evident that the creation and subsequent history of EFTA is closely linked to the EC. Although EFTA was formed as a reaction to the EC, trade co-operation with the EC developed as time went by. In 1973, the year in which the United Kingdom and Denmark joined the EC, free trade agreements came into force between the remaining EFTA members and the EC, thus creating a free trade area covering almost the whole of Western Europe, at least for most industrial products.

The close ties between EFTA and the EC are also apparent from the fact that the EC is by far the most important trading partner for all individual EFTA countries, much more important than the EFTA partners as a group.

In 1984 plans were produced for more far-reaching European co-operation, with the Luxembourg Declaration stating that this co-operation should lead to a dynamic European Economic Space. This Luxembourg process, as it was known, was given a new dimension following publication in 1985 of the White Paper on the completion of the internal market in the EC and the subsequent adoption of the Single European Act. EFTA will need to join in this process if it is not to be left behind in the trade integration process in the EC, and to prevent the consequent undermining of the importance of the free trade agreements. In 1989 the President of the European Commission, Jacques Delors, gave added impetus in this direction by an address to the European Parliament. Between 1989 and 1991 there were intensive negotiations on the creation of what is now referred to as the European Economic *Area* (EEA). In October 1991 agreement was reached on the creation of that area with effect from 1

January 1993. The agreement aimed to extend to the EFTA countries the 'four freedoms' (free movement of goods, services, capital and persons) to be achieved within the EC as a result of Project 1992. The legislation applicable, for instance in the sphere of competition, is largely the legislation in force in the EC. However, the EEA does not go so far as the EC's internal market: thus, border formalities will be retained because trade policy in relation to third countries is not being harmonised, but the formalities will be greatly simplified.

Progress towards the EEA was twice delayed. The first time this was caused by a judgement of the EC Court of Justice concerning the proposed joint EEA Court, which prompted amendment of the agreement. The second delay was due to the Swiss referendum which voted against joining the EEA, so that it could not be launched on 1 January 1993 but only a year later, without Switzerland.

The Luxembourg process comprises not only trade policy co-operation but also co-operation on statistics, small and medium-sized enterprises and education. Thus in 1991 agreement was reached on the expansion of the EC student exchange ERASMUS (European Action Scheme for the Mobility of University Students) to include students from EFTA countries.

Further changes to EFTA took place on 1 January 1995 as a number of members – Austria, Finland and Sweden – have become members of the EU. This means that there is little left of EFTA in the end.

6.4 Regional economic integration in North America

The first step in the process of regional economic integration in North America was taken in 1965 with the conclusion of the US–Canada Automotive Agreement, often known as the US–Canada Auto Pact, for short. One outcome of this was tariff-free trade in motor vehicles and parts between the US and Canada. A few years later, with the development of the *maquiladores*, bilateral trade between the US and Mexico began to expand. *Maquiladores* are businesses in Mexico, mainly along the US border to begin with, which process or assemble parts imported from the US and subsequently export them to the US. The customs rules are such that the US customs only charge import duties on the value added in Mexico and not on the total value of the goods, as normally happens.

After a lull on the regional economic integration front in North America, there have been extensive negotiations since 1985, leading to a series of bilateral agreements, the most important being the US–Canada Free Trade Agreement of 1988. This agreement provides for the gradual elimination of import duties and quotas over a ten-year period from 1 January 1989 and a reduction in barriers to trade in services and direct investments. In the agriculture sector, a ban was agreed on export subsidies in bilateral trade. Government procurement policy has also been liberalised by both sides, and mechanisms created for resolving disputes via binding verdicts. The two countries regard various aspects of the agreement as a possible model for multilateral agreements in the GATT Uruguay Round.

Box 6.1: NAFTA WE HAFTA

President Bill Clinton had to wage an intensive campaign in order to get the NAFTA Treaty accepted by the American Congress in time. He demonstrated his viewpoint by appearing in a baseball cap bearing the words 'NAFTA WE HAFTA'.

Clinton's principal opponent in the NAFTA debate was his former rival in the presidential election campaign, Ross Perot, who expects NAFTA to cause many American jobs to disappear to Mexico with what he calls a 'giant sucking sound'. Perot's lobby suffered severely after Perot made a poor showing in a television debate with Vice President Al Gore. However, the many concessions which President Clinton had to make in order to win over Congress played a more important part in the battle for parliamentary approval of NAFTA. Side-deals were made in order to cushion the producers of items such as sugar, tomatoes and citrus fruits, but other types of concession were also necessary. The most telling example was that of South California, where a Congressman actually managed to secure a complete development bank for the border area with Mexico, with a working capital of $252 million, in exchange for his vote in favour of NAFTA – evidently under the motto of 'one bank, one vote'.

It is not yet possible to make any definite comments on the effects of the free trade agreement between the US and Canada, as the transitional period is still not over. However, it does look reasonably likely that the countries concerned can reap the potential advantages without significant negative effects on other countries as a result of trade diversion. Little trade diversion is likely to result from Canadian suppliers forcing other exporters out of the US market, since the American tariffs which have now been abolished for Canadian exporters were low anyway. Although Canadian tariffs are higher so that, in principle, more trade diversion is possible here, the significance of the Canadian market in total world trade is so small that the quantitative importance of this trade diversion will probably be limited.

The next and hitherto most important step in the integration process in North America was the conclusion of a North American Free Trade Agreement (NAFTA), in which the US, Canada and Mexico participate. The negotiations began in June 1991, the objective being to eliminate restrictions on movements of goods, services and direct investments between the three countries and to protect intellectual property rights (such as patents and copyrights). The negotiations were concluded in August 1992 with the establishment of a draft agreement: NAFTA was launched on 1 January 1994 and the intention is that it should be implemented over a ten- to fifteen-year period. In the US, in particular, ratification of the treaty by the House of Representatives proved difficult: this is because of NAFTA's special characteristics compared with other free trade agreements, it being an agreement between two highly developed industrial countries and a country which is substantially less developed. For instance, there are fears in the US that competition from Mexico will lead to job losses; it is sometimes claimed that the competition would be 'unfair' because social standards, such as the ban on child labour, are not always respected in Mexico. Nevertheless, empirical research by the Institute for International Economics in Washington DC suggests that there will actually be a net gain in jobs in the US because exports to Mexico will also expand.[5]

Another controversial issue in the debate was the environmental aspect of NAFTA. In the US, many people fear that the less stringent environmental standards would prompt American companies to move to Mexico, thus causing damage, or further damage, to the environment there, and adding to the negative social consequences of NAFTA. Once the new American President Clinton had concluded side agreements in the social and environmental sphere, the NAFTA Treaty was approved by Congress in November 1993.

6.5 Regional economic integration between developing countries

Following the example of regional economic integration processes in Europe, attempts at integration have also been made in developing countries. In general it can be said that these attempts were associated with various problems and were unsuccessful in many cases. This section will consider regional economic integration in Latin America, Africa and Asia and the Middle East respectively (for the countries belonging to the various integration arrangements see Tables 6.2, 6.3 and 6.4), before giving a brief account of the reasons for the lack of success.

In Latin America the process of regional economic integration began in the 1950s. The underlying philosophy was in accordance with the strategy of industrialisation by import substitution, which was current in Latin America at the time: this meant directing industrialisation at the production of industrial goods to replace imports. One disadvantage of this strategy is that many countries in the region have a domestic market which is too small to allow efficient production of the goods concerned. Regional free trade was meant to solve this problem by also permitting production for the markets of partner countries in the integration arrangement. This was a major consideration in the formation of the Latin American Free Trade Association (LAFTA) and the Central American Common Market (CACM), both set up in 1961. The late 1960s and early 1970s brought the Andean Pact, uniting a number of LAFTA countries, and the Caribbean Community (CARICOM). In 1980, LAFTA gave way to the Latin American Integration Association (LAIA). One of the most important recent steps in Latin America was the 1991 agreement on the formation of the Mercado Comun del Sur (MERCOSUR) by Argentina, Brazil, Paraguay and Uruguay.

In Africa the history of regional integration is linked to decolonisation. Attempts were made to alleviate the associated problems by economic co-operation. A great

---

[5] G. C. Hufbauer and J. J. Schott, *North American Free Trade: Issues and Recommendations*, Washington DC, 1992, p. 337.

Table 6.2 Regional integration groupings in the western hemisphere (including only a selection of Caribbean countries)

	CACM	CARICOM	LAFTA/LAIA	MERCOSUR	ANDEAN Pact
Founded	1960	1973	1960/1980	1991	1969
Objective*	FTA	CU	FTA	FTA	FTA
Belize	x				
Costa Rica	x				
El Salvador	x				
Guatemala	x				
Honduras	x				
Nicaragua	x				
Panama	x				
Antigua and Barbuda		x			
Bahamas		x			
Barbados		x			
Dominica		x			
Grenada		x			
Jamaica		x			
Trinidad and Tobago		x			
Argentina			x	x	
Bolivia			x		x
Brazil			x	x	x
Chile			x		x
Colombia			x		x
Ecuador			x		
Guyana			x		
Paraguay			x	x	
Peru			x		x
Uruguay			x	x	
Venezuela			x		x

* FTA = free trade area, CU = customs union

Source: IMF Occasional Paper no. 93, 1992

many co-operation schemes were set up, but only the principal ones will be mentioned here. In West Africa the Economic Community of West African States (ECOWAS) was set up in 1975. In East and Southern Africa the Preferential Trade Area (PTA) has been in force since 1984. In Central Africa, negotiations are in progress on the amalgamation of two existing integration schemes, namely the Customs and Economic Union of Central Africa (UDEAC) and the Economic Community of the Great Lakes Countries (CEPGL).

In Asia and the Middle East, regional economic integration has not so far been as popular as in the regions discussed above. There was a very ambitious plan produced

Table 6.3 Regional integration groupings in Africa (selection only).

	CEPGL	ECOWAS	PTA	UDEAC
Founded	1976	1975	1981	1964
Objective*	FTA	FTA	FTA	FTA
Angola			x	
Benin		x		
Botswana			x	
Burkina Faso		x		
Burundi			x	
Cameroon				x
Central Africa Republic				x
Chad				x
Congo				x
Ethiopia				x
Gabon		x		
Ghana		x		
Guinea		x		
Ivory Coast		x		
Madagascar			x	
Mali		x		
Mauritania		x		
Mozambique			x	
Niger		x		
Nigeria		x		
Senegal		x		
Somalia			x	
Sudan			x	
Tanzania			x	
Uganda			x	
Zaire	x			
Zambia			x	
Zimbabwe			x	

* FTA = free trade area

Source: IMF Occasional Paper no. 93, 1992

by a number of Arab countries in 1964 for the formation of the Arab Common Market (ACM), but it was never really implemented. The best known integration scheme in Asia is the Association of South East Asian Nations (ASEAN), launched in 1967. Two other co-operative arrangements are the Economic Co-operation Organisation (ECO) of Iran, Pakistan and Turkey, and the Gulf Co-operation Council (GCC) of a number of Persian Gulf countries.

It is not possible to discuss the operation of all the above integration arrangements in this chapter: we shall just give a general description of the difficult

Table 6.4   Regional integration groupings in Asia (developing countries only)

	ASEAN	ACM	ECO**	GCC
Founded	1967	1964	1985	1981
Objective*	FTA	CU		CU
Brunei	x			
Indonesia	x			
Malaysia	x			
Philippines	x			
Singapore	x			
Thailand	x			
Bahrein				x
Egypt		x		
Iran				x
Iraq		x		
Jordan		x		
Kuwait				x
Libya		x		
Oman				x
Qatar				x
Saudi Arabia				x
Syria		x		
United Arab Emirates				x
Yemen				x
Pakistan			x	
Turkey			x	

* FTA = free trade area, CU = customs union
** The ECO aims to promote bilateral trade and co-operation in industrial planning.

Source: IMF Occasional Paper no. 93, 1992

progress of regional integration in developing countries and the possible reasons for that difficulty.

First, integration between developing countries often suffers from poor performance as regards implementation of the agreements made, although there are some variations here. On the one hand, there are the CACM and the GCC where the participating countries were relatively energetic in implementing the agreements; on the other hand, there are groups such as ECOWAS and UDEAC where the agreements were hardly implemented at all. One problem here is generally that trade is not automatically liberalised in accordance with a particular, pre-determined timetable, but via a system of 'positive lists'. This means that explicit agreement has to be reached on the products which are to be liberalised, creating a host of opportunities for delaying tactics.

If we consider the integration groupings from the point of view of the trend in intra-regional trade as a fraction of the members' total trade, we again find that there has

Table 6.5 Intra-regional exports, as a percentage of total exports of the region, for a number of integration groupings of developing countries; 1960–90.

Integration grouping	1960	1970	1975	1980	1985	1990
Andean Pact	0.7	2.0	3.7	3.8	3.4	4.6
ASEAN	4.4	20.7	15.9	16.9	18.4	18.6
CACM	7.0	25.7	23.3	24.1	14.7	14.8
CEPGL		0.4	0.3	0.1	0.8	0.6
ECOWAS		3.0	4.2	3.5	5.3	6.0
GCC		3.0	2.6	2.8	4.6	4.4
LAFTA/LAIA	7.9	9.9	13.6	13.7	8.3	10.6
PTA		8.4	9.4	8.9	7.0	8.5
UDEAC	1.5	5.0	2.7	1.7	2.1	4.6

Source: IMF Occasional Paper no. 93, 1992

not generally been any increase (see Table 6.5). An exception to this was the CACM during the first ten years of its existence (1960–70) and LAFTA in the period 1960–80. In the case of ASEAN, often seen as one of the most successful regional groupings of developing countries, intra-regional trade has actually declined considerably since the 1970s, although with 18.6 per cent of total trade in 1990, its share is certainly not insignificant. The reason is that the trade preferences which the ASEAN countries have granted to one another have so far been of minor importance. The preferential import tariffs are only 25 per cent lower than the tariffs for non-members; moreover, during the 1980s the preferential tariffs applied to only about 5 per cent of intra-ASEAN trade.[6] The success of ASEAN is therefore due mainly to the fact that the countries achieved a positive outcome by jointly conducting negotiations with OECD countries on economic matters.[7]

We have already referred to the lack of automatic progress in regional liberalisation as a factor which explains the laborious process of regional integration between developing countries. Another factor is that import tariffs in developing countries are often an important source of revenue for the government; this makes it difficult to abolish them. Difficulties were also caused by the debt problems of the developing countries in the 1980s, which on several occasions led to trade restrictions in order to combat the shortage of foreign exchange. The restrictions were often also applied to integration partners.

The most fundamental problem concerning regional economic integration between developing countries is the tension which has often existed between an import substitution policy and the establishment of regional trade policy co-operation. Import substitution creates vested interests in the import-competing sector which are difficult

[6] See V. Balasubramanyam, 'ASEAN and Regional Trade Co-operation in Southeast Asia', in D. Greenaway *et al.* (ed.), *Economic Aspects of Regional Trading Arrangements*, Hemel Hempstead, 1989, pp. 167–87, especially p. 172.
[7] See A. de la Torre and M. R. Kelly, *Regional Trade Arrangements*, Occasional Paper no. 93, International Monetary Fund, Washington DC, 1992, p. 28.

to overcome, even if it is 'only' a question of regional free trade. A minimum degree of external orientation is therefore necessary to open up markets. A very telling point here is that intra-regional trade grew faster in Asia than in the EC and North America in the 1980s, even though regional integration agreements are much less important in that part of the world.

Bibliography

Curzon, V., *The Essentials of Economic Integration: Lessons of EFTA Experience*, London, 1974.

De la Torre, A. and Kelly, M. R., *Regional Trade Arrangements*, Occasional Paper No. 93, IMF, Washington DC, 1992.

Greenaway, D. et al. (eds), *Economic Aspects of Regional Trading Arrangements*, Hemel Hempstead, 1989.

Hufbauer, G. C. and Schott, J. J., *North American Free Trade: Issues and Recommendations*, Washington DC, 1992.

Lintner, V. and Mazey, S., *The European Community: Economic and Political Aspects*, London, 1991.

Molle, W., *The Economics of European Integration*, Aldershot, 1990.

Pelkmans, J. and Winters, A., *Europe's Domestic Market*, London, 1988.

Publications

EU

Bulletin of the European Union. Monthly summary of the most important EU decisions.

EFTA

EFTA Annual Report 19 . . . [reporting year]. Report on the activities of EFTA.

Addresses

EU

European Commission
Rue de la Loi 200
1049 Brussels
Belgium

EFTA

European Free Trade Association
9-11 Rue de Varembé
1211 Geneva 20
Switzerland

7 Special institutional frameworks

7.1 Introduction

This chapter will look at special institutional frameworks for international trade, in the sense of arrangements which differ from what is normal in market economies using money. This concerns international trade between countries with a centrally planned economy, trade between market economies and centrally planned economies (East–West trade), and various forms of counter-trade.

7.2 COMECON

Regional economic integration has occurred not only in market economies but also between countries with a different economic system in the form of a centrally planned economy. This concerns mainly the Central and East European countries and the Soviet Union in the post-war period.

A feature of centrally planned economies is that the means of production are state-owned and the economic process is not controlled by market forces but by organs of the state. Control takes place via plans which set targets, particularly for production. As regards international trade, the state has a monopoly on transactions with other countries.

It will be obvious that regional economic integration between centrally planned economies is totally different from that between market economies. Mutual trade cannot be promoted by the elimination of tariffs and other trade barriers, because these have no effect at all on the volume of international trade. Mutual trade can therefore only be stimulated by co-ordination of the planning process following inter-governmental consultation between the various countries or by decision-making at supranational level. In the latter case, planning is transferred to a supranational level.

The history of regional economic integration for centrally planned economies began in the period immediately after World War II. In 1947 the consultations on Marshall Aid and economic co-operation with the East European countries and the Soviet Union broke down as a result of the rapidly deteriorating political relations between the Soviet Union and its former Western allies. This led to the division of Europe, with the West European countries, on the one hand, combining to form the Organisation for European Economic Co-operation in 1948 (see Chapter 3) and, on the other hand, the East European countries doing the same in 1949 in setting up the Council for Mutual Economic Assistance. In the West this organisation is often known as COMECON, an acronym based on its English name; in Eastern Europe itself the abbreviation CMEA is generally used in English. The founder members were Bulgaria, Hungary, Poland, Romania, the Soviet Union and Czechoslovakia. Albania joined within a month of its establishment; the German Democratic Republic was admitted in 1950. Later, non-European countries also joined, but will not be taken into account here.

Of the two economic integration options outlined for integration between centrally planned economies, inter-governmental consultation and supranational planning, the first was selected. That was in fact the only possible choice, because the split with the West at that time was motivated by fear that American hegemony would lead to loss of national sovereignty. It is necessary to be aware that, in practice, inter-governmental co-operation, in a grouping in which one partner – the Soviet Union – has a very dominant presence, can also easily jeopardise the sovereignty of the other partners. The choice between inter-governmental consultation and supranationality is a constantly recurring theme in the history of COMECON; for experience showed that the inter-governmental approach led to insoluble conflicts from time to time, particularly between the more industrialised members and those with a less developed industrial sector. The more developed countries were glad to see countries like Bulgaria and Romania concentrating more on agriculture, whereas those countries themselves wished to industrialise as well.

COMECON had a difficult start and continued to encounter problems subsequently. The initial period, 1949–54, was actually a dormant phase: although trade within the bloc did increase substantially during those years, this was due not to COMECON agreements but to bilateral agreements between member countries.

The next period (1955–63) was an active one, with COMECON gaining its Charter in 1961. In 1962 an important document was published on the principles of the 'socialist division of labour', with multilateral co-ordination of national plans as its central feature. The next phase comprising the rest of the 1960s can be called a period of stagnation: this was due in part to problems resulting from the non-convertibility of the members' currencies, in spite of efforts to resolve this problem in 1963 by setting up the International Bank for Economic Co-operation (IBEC) as a clearing institute. Here, mutual claims and debts resulting from trade transactions are balanced, leading to positions expressed in 'transferable roubles' as the unit of account. A country with a claim in transferable roubles could, in principle, use that for additional imports from the partner countries. However, the problem that establishment of the IBEC did not solve is that money (in this case a claim in terms of transferable roubles) cannot be converted into goods (commodity inconvertibility); i.e. it is not possible to use money to buy the goods one wants if those goods are not included (in sufficient quantity) in the central plan. This is one of the most fundamental problems of centrally planned economies.

During the 1970s COMECON was reactivated. Thus, in 1975 a joint plan was prepared for the integration of a number of sectors, including the petrochemical industry, agriculture and transport. The programme did actually lead to a number of industrial specialisation and co-operation projects, and stimulated intra-bloc trade in the products concerned, though in the end the number of products involved was small.

A special problem in mutual trade between centrally planned economies is the fixing of prices for trade transactions; because domestic prices are artificial and do not reflect the relative scarcity of goods, they are not a suitable basis for international trade transactions. For that reason, following a decision taken in Bucharest in 1958 in negotiations on trade contracts between COMECON countries, world market prices were used as the basis. Starting with the average past world market prices, a correction is applied in order to moderate the sometimes capricious fluctuations in prices on the 'capitalist' world market. This Bucharest formula was adapted in 1975 in that a five-year moving average of world market prices was subsequently taken as the basis. The change resulted mainly from the rise in the price of energy on Western markets: that price trend was now being reflected at an accelerated rate in intra-bloc trade. Here the Soviet Union was the main energy exporter while the other countries imported energy. Nevertheless, in practice the COMECON pricing system seems to have produced prices which were far too low, in relation to world market prices, for energy imported from the Soviet Union.

In the 1980s attempts were made to reform COMECON, but without success. One reason why reform was needed at the time was in order to link COMECON practices to the economic reforms which had already got under way in some countries before the turmoil of 1989. Following these events and the subsequent economic reforms in various countries, plus the loss of East Germany as a COMECON partner and the disintegration of the Soviet Union, mutual trade between the COMECON countries collapsed. Another factor here was the 1990 agreement whereby trade between member countries was to be paid for in hard currency at prevailing world market prices from 1 January 1991. This heralded the end of COMECON, which was formally terminated later in 1991, though bilateral agreements between COMECON partners for the settlement of trade transactions have been concluded in order to save at least part of the mutual trade.

7.3 East–West trade

The existence of countries with different economic systems, market-oriented or based on central planning, entails special problems in international trade between the countries concerned. This includes the problem of the different bodies dealing with international trade: private enterprises in the Western market economies and state agencies in the centrally planned economies of Eastern Europe. Another problem concerns the non-convertibility of the currencies of centrally planned economies. This means that those countries can only import from the West if they pay in Western currencies, which they have to earn by exporting to the West – and that is difficult,

Table 7.1   East–West trade: exports from West to East, 1955–90.

	1955	1960	1965	1970	1975	1980	1985	1990
In billions of US dollars	1.3	2.88	4.69	8.2	32.8	59.2	64.4	77.5
As a percentage of total exports by industrial countries	2.3	3.5	3.8	3.8	5.9	4.9	4.9	3.1
As a percentage of total imports by centrally planned economies	14.6	19.1	22.2	25.9	35.7	34.5	31.6	36

Source: GATT, *International Trade*, various issues

partly because of the often inferior quality of planned-economy products. Thus, the volume of East European exports to the West sets the ceiling on East–West trade, except for any trade based on Western credit (see later in this section).

Apart from economic complications, East–West trade is also greatly influenced by political factors. During the Cold War period, which began soon after World War II, both sides adopted measures to prevent East–West trade. The West imposed an embargo on exports of high technology products to East European countries via the COCOM (Co-ordinating Committee for Export Controls), particularly to prevent such products being used for military purposes. Imports from East European countries were also hindered by the introduction of barriers to trade in the form of quantitative restrictions specifically applicable to centrally planned economies. In the countries of Eastern Europe, major factors were the refusal to accept the offer of help under the Marshall Plan and the establishment of COMECON.

In the 1960s, East–West trade began to increase with the relaxation of the tension in political relations between East and West, as may be seen from Tables 7.1 and 7.2. The countries of Eastern Europe had a great need for imports from the West, particularly advanced technology products, because they were unable to develop these themselves, except in the military sector. More generally, the tables indicate that the quantitative significance of East–West trade is much greater for the East European countries than for Western countries.

In the 1970s East–West trade was further stimulated by the willingness of Western banks to grant loans to a number of East European countries as part of the process of recycling oil dollars which the oil-exporting countries had deposited with international banks. After the outbreak of the debt crisis in the early 1980s and the resulting need to cut imports from the West, East–West trade came under pressure once again. These trends are also evident from Tables 7.1 and 7.2.

In the trade policy sphere, too, some rapprochement took place, particularly during the 1980s. Although Poland, Romania and Hungary had already joined the GATT in

Table 7.2 East–West trade: exports from East to West, 1955–90.

	1955	1960	1965	1970	1975	1980	1985	1990
In billions of US dollars	1.7	2.78	4.63	7.65	24.3	57.1	59	90.9
As a percentage of total exports by centrally planned economies	18	18.5	21.3	23.3	28.4	32.3	28.1	36.8
As a percentage of total imports by industrial countries	3	3.5	3.8	3.6	4.3	4.3	4.4	3.6

Source: GATT, *International Trade*, various issues

1967, 1971 and 1973 respectively, this had little practical significance for the trade policy of the West towards these East European countries, because, in practice, the agreements concluded on the accession of the three countries (abolishing the quantitative restrictions specifically applicable to planned-economy countries) were only implemented very slowly. These restrictions in fact served as an extra precaution against dumping by the East European countries, in addition to the general rules on this (see Chapter 2). Dumping by centrally planned economies is more difficult to prove than that by market economies. The domestic price in the exporting country, which plays a key role in establishing dumping, is not a market price but a centrally fixed price in the case of a planned economy. Thus, the domestic price cannot be taken as a true reflection of production costs plus a reasonable profit margin, as it can in a market economy. A complicated procedure is therefore necessary to provide proof of dumping, the production costs in a market economy at a comparable level of development being taken as the criterion for the production costs in the centrally planned economy.

More important than accession to the GATT was the consultation between the European Community and COMECON which led to the Joint Declaration in 1988. This then opened the way to bilateral talks between the EC and individual members of COMECON. However, those agreements were fairly soon superseded by the trade liberalisation which took place after the upheavals of 1989. The first important measure was the PHARE Programme (*Pologne/Hongrie: Assistance à la Restructuration Economique*) of the Group of 24, the group of most developed countries in the world. Initially this programme was aimed at Poland and Hungary, but was soon extended – in 1990 – to include other countries of Eastern Europe. The programme is co-ordinated by the European Commission. Under PHARE, quantitative restrictions specifically applicable to the East European countries were abolished and these countries were brought into the Generalised System of Preferences (see Chapter 3), thus granting them preferential tariffs on their exports to developed industrial countries. A next important step was the conclusion of the Europe Agreements, which were association agreements, initially between the EC and Hungary, Poland and (what was then still) Czechoslovakia and later also Bulgaria and Romania, which were to lead to further trade liberalisation. However, there were exceptions for a number of 'sensitive' sectors such as agriculture, steel and textiles/clothing.

The other side of East–West trade, exports from West to East, also underwent liberalisation after 1989. For the East European countries, this meant liberalising imports to bring their economies into contact with the world market and thus also to introduce competition to the domestic market. For the West, it meant lifting export restrictions under the COCOM, though this happened somewhat later, at the end of 1993.

The effects of the changes which have taken place since 1989 are obvious in the trends in East–West trade where, as we see from Tables 7.1 and 7.2, exports from East European countries to the West increased particularly dramatically. In the opposite direction, growth was less marked, partly because the East European countries were hit by recession following the upheavals and the implementation of economic reforms, and this depressed demand, including demand for imports.

7.4 Counter-trade

Counter-trade involves some kind of direct link between exports to and imports from a particular country. Various arrangements are possible here.

Pure barter. This is the archetype of exchange, found in economies without any money. Goods are exchanged directly for one another in transactions which are agreed case by case. Nowadays, this form is no longer common, having been replaced by a number of more refined techniques, some of which will be discussed here.

Counter-purchase transactions. This is the commonest form of counter-trade, in which exporters are obliged to buy goods in order to sell their own goods. There need be no connection between the goods forming the two parts of the transaction. Purchase and counter-purchase often take place at different times because the counter-purchase generally extends over a longer period.

Buy-back transactions. This type of transaction is similar to counter-purchase transactions. The essential difference is that, in the case of buy-back transactions, there is a connection between the goods concerned in the two sides of the transaction. For example, the transaction may involve a machinery exporter being obliged to buy the products made with the machines in question. Other differences compared to counter-purchase transactions are that the amounts involved are larger and the contract periods are longer.

Owing to the lack of information about opportunities for counter-trade transactions, intermediaries have developed in this market. Thus, for example, there are business-es which specialise in dealing with counter-trade transactions. There are also 'barter clubs', in which businesses involved in counter-trade collaborate in obtaining infor-mation, e.g. on businesses which might be able to take over a compensation obligation.

Counter-trade occurs primarily in international trade between East and West, mutual trade within the former Eastern bloc, and trade between Western countries and developing countries or between developing countries themselves. This type of trade is very rare in trade between Western countries, apart from compensation orders in the military sphere.

The (former) centrally planned economies and developing countries generally enter into counter-trade for the purpose of overcoming the structural shortage of convertible foreign exchange. One reason for this shortage is the difficulty of sell-ing their own export products on the world market. Counter-trade transactions make it possible to use the marketing expertise of the trading partner or the latter's agent in order to sell the export products. The fact that the countries concerned are often not deemed sufficiently creditworthy to obtain commercial credit from the international banking system, and are thus dependent on this form of trade, plays a part too.

Another consideration which plays a role in counter-trade, particularly for oil-exporting developing countries, is that it offers a disguised means of evading mutual production-and-price agreements. This was and is particularly common among the poorer oil producers within this group.

It is difficult to estimate the quantitative importance of counter-trade, partly because this type of transaction is often not recorded as such and is thus concealed in the overall international trade figures. The International Monetary Fund[1] puts the proportion of world trade at a maximum of 10 per cent in the mid-1980s. It is often assumed that the quantitative importance of counter-trade has been declining since then. For the most recent period, since the turmoil of 1989 in Eastern Europe, another factor has been the economic reforms in those countries which include moving towards currency convertibility.

International institutions such as the IMF and the GATT are very inclined to point to the negative aspects of counter-trade. That is understandable since their function is to promote the multilateral trade and payments system. Counter-trade is a form of bilateralism and, as such, it has the associated drawbacks, particularly failure to make full use of trade potential because this type of trade, by its nature, precludes trade imbalances, even if these should obviously be present on the basis of compar-ative advantages. Moreover, counter-trade is an expensive form of trade because of the involvement of intermediaries who naturally wish to be paid for their services. Counter-trade must therefore be seen mainly as a way in which countries can still engage in trade under sub-optimum conditions, such as the lack of currency con-vertibility.

---

[1] International Monetary Fund, *Developments in International Exchange and Trade Systems*, World Economic and Financial Surveys, Washington DC, September 1989, p. 33.

7.5 The future

As was already indicated in the preceding sections of this chapter, the particular institutional frameworks arising from the special nature of trade found among centrally planned economies are on the way out, as a result of the ongoing transition of most of these economies to market economies. This is one of the tendencies important in shaping the international trade system of the future.

Another important development signalling the further liberalisation of world trade is the successful completion of the Uruguay Round of the GATT, which opened the door for the new World Trade Organisation (as was mentioned in Chapter 2).

There are, however, also movements working in the opposite direction which could intensify protectionism throughout the world. The most important development here is the creation of more regional trade groupings which may evolve into inward-looking, protectionist blocs. Chapter 6 was devoted to this aspect of the international trade system.

It is hard to predict which of the tendencies mentioned above will predominate in shaping the future international trading system. One statement that can safely be made, however, is that the process of trade liberalisation – whose path has been full of obstacles in the past – will encounter just as many in the future.

Bibliography

Banks, G., 'The Economics and Politics of Countertrade', *The World Economy*, 6, 1983, pp. 159–82.

International Monetary Fund, *Developments in International Exchange and Trade Systems*, World Economic and Financial Surveys, IMF, Washington DC, 1989.

Kaser, M., *COMECON: Integration Problems of the Planned Economies*, London, 1985.

Kelly, M. *et al.*, *Issues and Developments in International Trade Policy*, World Economic and Financial Surveys, IMF, Washington DC, August 1992, especially Chapter IV.

Robson, P., *The Economics of International Integration*, London, 1987.

Van Brabant, J. M., *Economic Integration in Eastern Europe: A Handbook*, Hemel Hempstead and New York, 1989.

Glossary

Key terms

Adjustment fatigue Indicates that a country has had to take so many measures to improve the economy that there is now strong resistance to any more adjustment.

Agreed minutes Outcome of negotiations in the *Paris Club*.

Anti-dumping Code A *GATT* agreement governing national anti-dumping procedures, first drawn up during the *Kennedy Round* and later revised in the *Tokyo Round*. The code was binding for the signatories but not automatically binding for all *GATT* countries.

Anti-dumping duties Compensating import duties which, under the *GATT* rules, may be applied if an investigation shows that dumping is going on and is causing or threatening *material injury* to the domestic industry in the importing country.

Arm's length principle Principle according to which multinational corporations base their *transfer prices* on the market prices for the products in question.

Article IV consultation Analysis of the economic situation in a member country made by the *IMF* staff.

Articles of Agreement Statutes of the *IMF*.

ASEAN Association of South East Asian Nations. Co-operation grouping, set up in 1967, which now includes Brunei, Indonesia, Malaysia, Philippines, Singapore and Thailand and has as one of its aims the creation of a *free trade area*.

Bail out the banks In the context of the debt problem, the expression means that a debtor country can pay the commercial banks more since the official debt has been restructured.

Baker plan Plan, proposed in 1985 by the American Treasury Secretary James Baker, which sought a solution to the *debt crisis* in structural reforms, on the assumption that the root of the problem was a liquidity crisis.

Balance-of-payments adjustment Change in economic relations, generally as a result of policy measures, which leads to an improvement in the balance of payments.

Beggar-thy-neighbour policy General term for a type of economic policy prevalent in the 1930s under which countries tried to pass on their own economic problems to their trading partners.

83

Blending A combination of financing resources (for example, using resources from both *ordinary funds* and *special funds*).

Board of Executive Directors See *Executive Board*.

Board of Governors Formal governing body of international financial institutions like the *IMF* and *World Bank* which includes a representative from each member country.

Brady plan Initiative, launched in 1989 by the American Treasury Secretary James Brady, which introduced debt reduction and *debt service* reduction as a solution to the *debt crisis*, thereby recognising that the problem was rooted in a solvency crisis.

Bretton Woods institutions Term applied to the *International Monetary Fund* and the *World Bank*, institutions founded at Bretton Woods in the United States.

Bretton Woods system International system of fixed exchange rates based on gold parities. The system lasted from 1944 to 1971.

Bridging loan Very short-term credit extended to the central banks of countries with liquidity problems to bridge over the period between a loan from one of the international financial institutions being agreed and the loan actually being disbursed.

Brundtland Commission The official name is the World Commission for Environment and Development. Its report on the relation between environment and development, issued in 1987, was subsequently adopted by the *UNEP* as a guideline for further action. An important feature of the report is the concept of *sustainable development*.

Buffer stock System that can be used to stabilise commodity prices. The buffer stock manager sells or buys, depending on whether the price is too high or too low.

Burden-sharing In the *IMF*, this term is applied to the system under which debtor countries pay a higher rate of interest and the remuneration received by creditor countries is reduced with the aim of building up reserves to protect the financial position of the *IMF* against arrears of payment (including interest foregone).

CACM Central American Common Market. Economic co-operation grouping of Central American countries, set up in 1961, whose aim, contrary to what the name suggests, is the establishment of a *free trade area*.

COCOM Co-ordinating Committee for Export Controls. A body on the basis of which, after the Second World War, the Western countries organised a embargo on exports of strategic goods to the East European countries. The committee was dissolved in 1994.

Cocos Co-ordination Commission Development Co-operation.

Code of Conduct on Transnational Corporations Document laying down rules of conduct regarding *multi- or transnational corporations*. The UN has been deliberating on such a code of conduct for a long time, but so far in vain. However, the *OECD* has guidelines for multinational corporations .

Co-financing The financing of a project by several official and/or commercial institutions.

COMECON Council for Mutual Economic Assistance, for which the English acronym CMEA was also used, especially in the region itself. This was the economic co-operation grouping for countries with a centrally planned economy, set up in

1949. The original members were Bulgaria, Czechoslovakia, Hungary, Poland, Romania and the Soviet Union. A year afterwards they were joined by the German Democratic Republic. Later, membership was extended to a number of non-European countries. The organisation was dissolved in 1991. The institution was obligated to extend the promised credit if the borrowing country met the performance criteria.

Committee of Alternates (of the *EMI* Council) Consisting mostly of the same central bank directors as sit on the *Monetary Committee*, it prepares the work of the *EMI* Council.

Commodity agreements Agreements aimed at influencing the commodity markets. These agreements may be concluded between producer countries only or between producer and consumer countries.

Commodity price instability Tendency for commodity prices to fluctuate sharply over time. This is connected with the generally low elasticities of demand for and supply of the commodities concerned.

Common Agricultural Policy Common policy of the *EU* countries aimed at ensuring a reasonable standard of living in the agricultural sector, stable markets, higher productivity in agriculture and a secure supply of agricultural products, while maintaining fair prices for the consumer.

Common market Form of regional trade policy co-operation involving the abolition of tariffs and other restraints on trade between participants, the pursuit of a common trade policy with respect to third countries and free movement of production factors between member countries.

Competitive devaluations The situation which occurs when several countries devalue their currencies with a view to gaining a competitive advantage over each other. Such a policy is an example of a *beggar-thy-neighbour policy*.

Concerted lending Orchestrated lending, for example the bank lending co-ordinated by the *IMF* during the *debt crisis*.

Concessional facility Facility under which credit is extended on considerably more favourable terms than is usual on the international capital markets.

Conditionality Among international financial institutions, the tying of economic conditions or *performance criteria* to the commitment and disbursement of credit.

Consensus on Officially Supported Export Credits A 1978 gentleman's agreement between the *OECD* countries in which they undertook to exercise restraint in their mutual competition over subsidies on export credits.

Constituency A group of member countries of an international institution which all vote for the same *Executive Director* and are represented in the institution by that director.

Countertrade Trade in which, in one way or another, a direct link is established between exports to and imports from a particular country. There are various possibilities such as simple barter, but countertrade mainly takes the form of counter-purchase transactions in which the exporter undertakes to purchase goods in return. The latter also applies to buy-back transactions, with the additional feature that a relation exists between the exported and the imported goods.

Credit tranche policy The basis of *IMF* credit policy. A loan is advanced not in a single lump sum but in a number of tranches equal to 25 per cent of the quota, the country being required to meet certain *performance criteria* in order to qualify for the disbursement of a tranche.

Customs union Form of regional trade policy co-operation involving the mutual abolition of tariffs and other trade barriers and the pursuit of a common trade policy with respect to third countries.

Cut-off date Debts incurred beyond this date are not included in the restructuring.

DAC Development Assistance Committee. Body set up in 1961 within the framework of the *OECD* to enable members to co-ordinate their efforts in the field of development aid and critically examine each other's policies through 'confrontations'.

Debt crisis Financial crisis dating from 1982 which endangered the international financial system because a number of developing countries (especially in Latin America) were no longer able to fulfil their foreign debt obligations.

Debt restructuring See *rescheduling*.

Debt service Obligation upon debtors to pay interest and principal.

Debt service ratio Ratio of foreign debt service obligations to exports of goods and services.

Development Committee Joint ministerial committee of governors of the *IMF* and the *World Bank* set up in 1974 to supervise the transfer of real resources to the developing countries.

Donor groups/support groups These groups co-ordinate the bilateral financial efforts on behalf of a particular country.

Double-majority voting procedure *GEF* voting procedure according to which projects must be approved both by a majority of the developing countries and a majority of the donor countries.

Drawing Portion of the loan on which the borrowing country can make a call provided that it satisfies certain conditions.

Dumping The selling of a product on a foreign market at less than the normal value, the usual measure of which is the domestic price in the exporting country.

East–West trade General term for international trade between countries with a centrally planned economy (East) and countries with a market economy (West).

Economic and Monetary Union (EMU) An integral part of *European Union* requiring the EMU participants to adopt a common monetary policy, link their currencies firmly together and harmonise their economic policies.

Economic Policy Committee *EU* committee of representatives of the ministries of finance and economic affairs which establishes guidelines for medium-term economic policy.

ECU European Currency Unit. European unit of account, reserve asset and numeraire based on a basket of *EU* currencies weighted according to economic importance.

EEA European Economic Area. Co-operative agreement between the *EU* and *EFTA*, excluding Switzerland, within which by 1994 the *four freedoms* of the integrated market in the *EU* will be extended to the *EFTA* countries, with the exception of Switzerland.

EFTA European Free Trade Association. *Free trade area* established in 1960 with an original membership consisting of Denmark, Norway, Austria, Portugal, United Kingdom, Sweden and Switzerland. In 1973, Denmark and the United Kingdom joined the *EC*, to be followed in 1986 by Portugal. Finland, Iceland and Liechtenstein were successively admitted as new members of EFTA.

Europe Agreements Association agreements between the *EU* and, initially, (the then) Czechoslovakia, Hungary and Poland and, later, Bulgaria and Romania, concluded following the 1989 upheavals in Eastern Europe and aimed at mutual trade liberalisation (although exceptions are made for 'sensitive' sectors).

European Act Amendment of the Treaties of Rome adopted in 1986 under which the process leading to an internal market was given a legal framework, the sphere of application of the treaties was extended to include foreign policy, and the decision-making process was modified (greater participation of the European Parliament, possibility of Council decisions concerning the *internal market* being taken by majority voting).

European Atomic Energy Community Community set up by the *ECSC* countries in 1957 for the purpose of overseeing the production and use of atomic energy in the European context.

European Central Bank (ECB) Central bank which, in the third stage of *EMU*, will be responsible for the everyday implementation of the common monetary policy and for the interlinked currencies.

European Coal and Steel Community (ECSC) Community set up in 1951 by Germany, France, Italy, Belgium, Netherlands and Luxembourg for the purpose of overseeing the production and consumption of coal and steel in the European context and creating free trade in these products.

European Community (EC) Community which resulted from the amalgamation, in 1967, of the *EEC*, the *ECSC* and Euratom.

European Economic Community (EEC) Community set up in 1957 by the *ECSC* countries for the purpose of creating a *common market* with unimpeded movement of goods, services, capital and persons and establishing a common economic policy and regulations.

European Monetary Co-operation Fund (EMCF) Fund into which all the European central banks participating in the *EMS* have transferred 20 per cent of their gold and dollar reserves in the form of revolving swap agreements, in exchange for which they have received ECUs. The Fund provides for the mutual settlement of intervention debts.

European Monetary Institute (EMI) Set up on 1 January 1994 to prepare, during the second stage, the final stage of *EMU*.

European Monetary System (EMS) A framework established by the *EU* countries to promote exchange rate stability in Europe. The *ERM* forms part of this system.

European Political Union Far-reaching political co-operation among the *EU* countries in a number of areas, including foreign policy, defence and justice.

European System of Central Banks Consists of the *ECB* and the national central banks and will determine monetary policy in the third stage of *EMU*.

European Union (EU) Union embracing the *EC*, *EMU* and *European Political Union* created in 1993 with the entry into force of the Maastricht Treaty.

Exchange Rate Mechanism (ERM) The *EMS* mechanism by means of which, on the basis of fixed but adjustable parities, the participating exchange rates are kept within set limits, with an obligation to intervene if the rate threatens to exceed those limits.

Executive Board A body delegated by the *Board of Governors* of an international financial institution to determine its day-to-day policy.

Executive Director A person delegated by one or more member countries to represent them in the day-to-day management of an international financial institution.

Export quota's System that can be used to stabilise the price of a commodity. A certain volume of exports is allocated to each of the participating exporting countries.

Exposure Loans outstanding.

Fast-disbursing credits 'Ready money', credits that can be quickly disbursed.

Financing gap Means that additional financing is necessary on top of an *IMF* loan in order to be able to implement an *IMF* programme.

Four freedoms Freedom of movement for goods, services, capital and persons.

Franco-German financial and economic co-operation council A formal body set up in 1988 within which the French and German finance ministers and central bank governors meet four times a year to consult on financial and economic matters.

Free-trade area Form of regional trade policy co-operation in which tariffs and other barriers to mutual trade are eliminated, without the adoption of a common trade policy with respect to third countries.

GATT General Agreement on Tariffs and Trade. This agreement was concluded in 1947 and, more or less, took the place of the proposed International Trade Organisation, which finally failed to materialise. On 1 January 1995 the GATT was incorporated into the World Trade Organisation (WTO).

Gearing ratio The ratio of loans outstanding to own funds (capital and reserves).

General Arrangements to Borrow (GAB) A 1962 loan agreement concluded with the *IMF* by the *Group of Ten* and Saudi Arabia under which the Fund can finance credit if its own resources are insufficient.

Generalised System of Preferences (GSP) System that resulted from negotiations in the framework of *UNCTAD*, involving the application of preferential tariffs to imports from developing countries by (groups of) industrialised countries.

Global Environmental Facility (GEF) Facility set up in 1990 by the World Bank and the *UNEP* for the purpose of improving the environment in developing countries.

Global financing Provision of credit by one financial institution via another, usually local, financial institution.

Group of Five Informal group (precursor of the G7) set up in 1967 and consisting of the ministers of finance and central bank governors of the five most important countries (United States, Japan, Germany, France and United Kingdom) who met to discuss current exchange-rate and interest-rate developments.

Group of Seven Informal group of the seven most important countries (United States, Canada, Japan, Germany, France, United Kingdom and Italy) which meets to consult on various matters. First met in 1976.

Group of Ten Group of eleven countries which participate in the *General Arrangements to Borrow* (United States, Canada, Japan, Germany, France, United Kingdom, Italy, Netherlands, Belgium, Sweden and Switzerland). Saudi Arabia, which also participates in the *GAB*, is an associate member.

Group of 24 (developing countries) Group set up in 1972 to which Africa, Central and South America and Asia each contribute eight representatives. The group discusses matters of concern to the developing countries in advance of meetings of the *Interim committee* and *Development Committee*.

Group of 24 (industrialised countries) Group of 24 industrialised (*OECD*) countries which, under the presidency of the European Commission, co-ordinates aid for Eastern Europe.

Group of 77 Group of developing countries which, particularly in the 1970s, played an important part as a promoter of developing country interests. In the course of time has grown into a much bigger group.

Guarantee capital Own funds (total capital stock plus reserves).

Guidelines for Multinational Corporations Recommendation addressed to multinational corporations operating in the *OECD* area by the joint governments of the *OECD* countries. These guidelines, adopted by the *OECD* in 1976, include, among other things, the *arm's length principle* and the principle of *national treatment* of foreign enterprises.

Headroom The room available for disbursing promised loans.

Helsinki package Comprises an amendment, agreed in 1991, to the *Consensus on Officially Supported Export Credits* aimed at separating trade transactions financed by (tied) development aid from commercially viable transactions. The aim was twofold. On the one hand, to ensure that development aid produces additional resources for the recipient countries and, on the other, to restrain the mutual competition over export subsidies.

Imminent default Indicates that in the near future a country will be unable to meet its debt and *debt service* obligations and is a candidate for a *Paris Club* settlement.

Infant-industry argument Argument for giving temporary protection to a newly established industry.

Integrated or internal market Form of regional economic co-operation which eliminates all barriers to the cross-border movement of goods, services, capital and labour. A common trade policy is applied with respect to non-participants.

Integrated Programme for Commodities Idea put forward within the context of the *NIEO* in the UN framework to improve the position of commodity exporters. Among other things, a Common Fund for financing a series of buffer stocks was to have been set up.

Interim Committee Most important policy-making body of the *IMF*, set up in 1974 and consisting of the ministers of the same 24 countries as have seats on the *Board of Executive Directors*.

Internal market See *integrated or internal market*.

International Bank for Reconstruction and Development (IBRD) See *World Bank*.

International Development Association (IDA) Part of the *World Bank group*. Set up in 1960 to provide concessional credit for the purpose of promoting the economic development of the poorest countries.

International Energy Agency (IEA) An organisation, set up in 1974 under the auspices of the *OECD* but in practice autonomous, which drew up a common energy programme in order to reduce the dependence of the *OECD* countries on imported petroleum from the *OPEC* countries.

International Finance Corporation (IFC) Financing institution established in 1956 as part of the *World Bank group* to promote private enterprise in the developing countries.

International Monetary Fund (IMF) Monetary institution set up to oversee the *international monetary system*.

International Monetary system The system of international exchange rates.

Kennedy Round (1963–1967) Round of *GATT* negotiations in which considerable progress was made with the reduction of import tariffs.

LAFTA/LAIA Latin American Free Trade Association/Latin American Integration Association. An economic co-operation grouping of South American countries set up in 1960 and reorganised under a new name in 1980. The aim is to create a *free trade area*.

Lender of last resort Central bank on which the commercial banks can fall back if they have liquidity problems.

Linear-reductions approach *GATT* negotiating technique concerning tariff reductions first applied in the *Kennedy Round*. The starting point is a uniform percentage tariff reduction so that subsequently it is only necessary to negotiate over products to which exceptions are to apply.

Liquidity position Ratio of liquid assets (uncommitted general resources) to liquid liabilities (loans outstanding and reserve tranche positions).

Local payment A payment which the debtor has made in local currency but which is not yet at the disposal of the creditor because in the debtor's country there is not enough foreign exchange available.

London Club or London agreements Steering group consisting of a number of the bigger banks which represent the whole of the commercial banking system.

Managing Director (MD) Chairman of the IMF's *Executive Board* and head of the *IMF* staff.

Market conformity of tariffs Import tariffs may affect the market process, but they leave the operation of the market intact in the sense that foreign competition is not excluded. This is an important consideration behind the GATT's preference for tariffs as a trade policy instrument.

Marshall aid American assistance for European reconstruction after the Second World War. Named after the then American Secretary of State George C. Marshall who announced America's intention to provide the aid in 1947.

Material injury caused by dumping An important criterion in the *GATT* rules concerning the possibility of retaliation against dumping. The *Anti-dumping Code* which emerged from the *Tokyo Round* requires the determination of material injury to be based on the volume of the dumped imports and their effect on domestic prices in the importing country.

Monetary character of the IMF An expression used to indicate that the Fund is built up from central bank reserves and that *IMF* lending involves reserve creation.

Monetary Committee *EU* committee composed of senior officials from the ministries of finance and national central bank directors which, under the treaty, is responsible for overseeing capital movements and balance-of-payments developments and, in practice, prepares almost all the decisions of the Ecofin Council.

Most-favoured-nation treatment *GATT* principle which implies that a country's various trading partners receive the same trade policy treatment.

Multilateral contract System used to stabilise commodity prices. When the maximum price is reached, the producer countries are required to make available agreed amounts of the commodity. When the minimum price is reached, the consumer countries are required to purchase agreed amounts.

Multilateral Investment Guarantee Agency (MIGA) Institution founded in 1988 for the purpose of promoting direct investment in the developing countries by providing guarantees against non-commercial risks.

Multilateral surveillance See *Surveillance*.

Multi- or transnational corporations Enterprises established in a number of countries. In the UN context they are always referred to as transnational corporations.

Multi-Year Rescheduling Agreement (MYRA) Restructuring of commercial debt so that the *debt service* obligations are spread over many years (fourteen in the case of Mexico).

NAFTA North American Free Trade Agreement. Framework within which Canada, Mexico and the United States have been co-operating since 1 January 1994 to establish a *free trade area*.

National treatment Principle relating to international trade and investment which requires foreign goods or companies to be treated in the same way as their domestic equivalents.

New International Economic Order (NIEO) Idea advanced by the developing countries in the 1970s and also taken up in the UN. The aim was to adapt the international economic order to developing country interests.

New protectionism Revival of protectionist tendencies in the course of the 1970s, especially in the form of trade policy measures in the non-tariff sphere. Many of these measures fall in the grey area not directly addressed by the formal *GATT* rules.

Non-discrimination The main principle of the *GATT* which finds expression in the *most-favoured-nation* principle and *national treatment* of imports.

OECD/OEEC Organisation for Economic Co-operation and Development/ Organisation for European Economic Co-operation. The non-communist European countries formed the second of these organisations in 1948, mainly for the purpose of organising *Marshall aid*. In 1961, the OEEC was replaced by the OECD which differs from the former with respect to both membership (Canada and the United States became full members) and range of activities (co-ordination of development aid was added). Later, other countries joined, among them Japan. In 1973 the membership stood at 24. Mexico became the 25th member in 1994.

OECD country reviews Annual review by the OECD's Economic and Development Review Committee of economic policy and economic developments in the member countries. Based on the *OECD* secretariat's country analyses, which are published as Country Surveys.

OECD forecast Forecast of economic developments in the *OECD* countries made by the *OECD* secretariat using the Interlink model. This is published in the twice-yearly '*Economic Outlook*'.

OECD policy dialogue The *OECD* provides a permanent forum for consultations on economic policy among those responsible for policy in the individual member countries.

OPEC Organisation of Petroleum Exporting Countries. Producer organisation embracing a number of oil-producing countries. Has operated as a *producer cartel*.

Ordinary funds Funds raised on the capital markets and used for non-concessional lending.

Paid-in capital The portion of the total contribution to the capital stock actually paid in.

Paris Club Meeting place mainly for developed creditor countries. Variable composition. Negotiates the settlement of government loans made to countries which are unable to meet their obligations in full.

Performance criteria Economic criteria on the basis of which the *IMF* tests the progress made with an adjustment programme and determines whether a country qualifies for the next drawing on the associated *IMF* loan.

Petrodollars Dollars earned from oil.

PHARE programme (Poland and Hungary – aid for economic restructuring) Programme set up by the *Group of 24* following the upheavals in Eastern Europe in 1989 and intended to support the transformation process in the countries concerned. The programme, which is co-ordinated by the European Commission, was very quickly extended to other East European countries in addition to the original pair: Poland and Hungary.

Polluter pays principle Principle adopted in 1974 within the framework of the *OECD* to prevent national environmental policy from distorting international competition.

Positive adjustment policy Concept developed by the *OECD* secretariat in the 1970s. Implies a positive approach to changes in international competitiveness, through measures that encourage the operation of markets and especially the labour market.

Principal supplier rule This rule formed the basis of the negotiating technique employed in the rounds of *GATT* negotiations which preceded the *Kennedy Round*. Countries negotiate with each other over products with respect to which they are the principal supplier on each other's markets.

Producer cartel Co-operative grouping of producers for the purpose of increasing revenues by forcing up the price of their product (see *OPEC*).

Qualified majority More than a fixed percentage of the votes, for example more than 85 per cent.

Quota Capital contributed by a member country to the *IMF*, expressed in *SDRs*.

Rating agency Commercial agency that assesses the creditworthiness of banks and financial institutions.

Reciprocity Trade policy principle with different interpretations. In the *GATT* it means exchanging equivalent trade policy concessions in negotiating rounds (first-difference reciprocity). The supporters of the idea of fair trade in the United States interpret the principle as mutual equivalent market access between countries across the board.

Regional economic commissions UN commissions in which the UN members in a specific region participate.

Remuneration The compensation (equal to the *SDR* interest less the *burden-sharing* surcharge) which the *IMF* pays countries whose currency is used for lending purposes.

Replenishment Additional payment of capital.

Rescheduling Establishment of a new schedule for the payment of principal and interest on debt.

Rescheduling period Period during which the *debt service* falling due is postponed.

Reserve tranche The portion of the quota that a country has paid in currencies and *SDRs* plus the portion of the quota being used for *IMF* lending. The reserve tranche is unconditionally drawable.

Revolving character of credit Expression used by the *IMF* to indicate that credit is relatively short-term and circulates among debtors, according to whether the situation is one of surplus or deficit.

Screwdriver plants Factories which derive their name from the fact that only very little value is added because virtually all the components come from elsewhere and are simply assembled. With this sort of plant it is possible to evade *anti-dumping duties*.

SDR (Special Drawing Right) International liquidity (reserve asset) created by the *IMF* and valued in terms of a basket of five currencies: dollar, yen, German mark, French franc and pound sterling.

Sherpas Senior officials.

Simple majority More than 50 per cent of the votes.

Solvency-free lending Lending with respect to which the commercial banks do not need to set aside any provisions.

Solvency ratio Risk-weighted liabilities divided by *guarantee capital*.

Special funds Funds obtained in the form of grants and used to finance soft loans.

STABEX *EC* compensatory financing system on behalf of former colonies in Africa, the Caribbean and the Pacific (ACP countries), set up under the Lomé Agreements.

Stand-by arrangement (SBA) *IMF* credit with maximum maturity of eighteen months.

Stock of debt Restructuring of a country's total *debt service* obligations, regardless of the period in which they fall.

Surveillance Overseeing exchange rates and national economic policy.

Sustainable development Defined by the *Brundtland Commission* as meeting the needs of the present generation without jeopardising the chances of future generations being able to meet theirs.

Terms of trade of commodities relative to manufactures Amount of industrial products which can be imported per unit of commodity exports. In developing country circles it is generally maintained that these terms of trade are tending to deteriorate.

Tokyo Round (1973–79) Round of *GATT* negotiations in which a serious start was made on the liberalisation of non-tariff trade barriers.

Trade creation An effect of regional trade policy co-operation reflecting the fact that new trade between the participants is generated because suppliers from member countries can now sell their goods more cheaply, thanks to the mutual abolition of restrictions on trade.

Trade diversion An effect of regional trade policy co-operation reflecting the fact that imports which previously came from countries not belonging to the integration association have been replaced by imports from a partner country which has benefited from the mutual abolition of restrictions on trade.

Transfer prices Prices set by multinational corporations for their internal transactions.

Transnational corporations See *Multi- or transnational corporations.*

Transparency of tariffs Import tariffs are a transparent trade policy instrument because foreign exporters can consult the tariff schedule of a country to which they (would like to) export and thus be certain about the tariffs they will have to pay. This, together with the *market conformity of tariffs*, was a consideration underlying the *GATT*'s preference for tariffs as a trade policy instrument.

Treaties of Rome The 1957 treaties which established the *EEC* and Euratom.

Triple-A status The highest possible rating available. Only accorded to the most solvent and trustworthy debtors.

UNCED United Nations Conference on Environment and Development. A conference held in Rio de Janeiro in the summer of 1992. Among other things, the conference produced, in Agenda-21, an extensive action programme for sustainable development in the 21st century, together with two treaties, one on climate change and the other on biodiversity.

UNCTAD United Nations Conference for Trade and Development. UN organisation, established in 1964, which works to uphold the position of the developing countries in the world economy.

UNCTC United Nations Centre on Transnational Corporations. This centre, set up in 1975, supports the work of the UN's Commission on Transnational Corporations, in particular by carrying out research.

UNEP United Nations Environmental Program. Set up in 1973, among other things, to promote international co-operation on the environment and to keep up with the development of the environmental situation worldwide.

Uruguay Round (1986–93) Round of *GATT* negotiations with the most ambitious agenda of all GATT-rounds, in particular because it included trade in agricultural products and services.

Wapenhans report Internal *World Bank* investigation which, among other things, found that increased lending had been achieved at the expense of the quality of the loan portfolio.

White paper on Completion of the internal market 1985 white paper in which the European Commission identified the physical, technical and fiscal obstacles to the creation of an internal market.

World Bank Financial institution whose aim is to promote economic and social progress in the developing countries by raising economic productivity. The name World Bank is sometimes applied to the *IBRD* only, but sometimes used to indicate the *IDA* and *IFC* as well.

World Bank group The *IBRD*, the *IFC* and the *IDA*.

Index